So *Now* What?

Fedd Books
P.O. Box 341973
Austin, TX 78734

www.thefeddagency.com

Published in association with The Fedd Agency, Inc., a literary agency.

ISBN: 978-1-957616-75-9

LCCN: 2024935594

Printed in the United States of America

To Ryan who always has a poop bag in his pocket. My restoration would not have been possible without you. Thank you from the bottom of my heart.

—Juli

My Ordeal of Huge Magnitude was breast cancer.

Yours might be cancer, too.

Or a natural disaster, or the loss of a loved one, or reimagining your career.

We all have them.

It's one of the things that unites us as humans.

In fact, none of us are immune to an ordeal of huge magnitude.

Use my voice to help find yours.

An Ordeal of Huge Magnitude

That's what my friend Linda called my cancer.

Everyone experiences ordeals of huge magnitude. And once we get to the other side, we are forever and inexplicably changed.

A week before Christmas, my ordeal of huge magnitude commenced. Deep down, when my boobs were being smashed into that mammogram machine, I already knew that things were about to change. What I didn't know—and couldn't know—was what the next few months would feel like.

And the thing about ordeals of huge magnitude is that while you are dealing with them, you are required to continue living.

As I write this, I am six months post-diagnosis. I have had two operations, countless doctor appointments, and menopause. I'm still struggling to find the right cocktail of supplements, and still hoping acupuncture, medical massage, and yoga will keep me moving forward. I'm trying to get to know this new me, continue to restore, and find my footing…all while still being a wife, a mom, a daughter, a sister, and a friend.

It is really fucking hard.

At seemingly benign moments, my mind replays moments in vivid detail—like a weird movie montage, scene by scene. Mammogram. Ultrasound. Diagnosis. Yada yada…

I remember every detail of my first pre-op room. The clock that ticked for one second, held in place for four, and then scurried to the fifth…only to repeat all over again. The teal, black, and gray scrubs and gowns—like some weird 1985 show choir. My husband Ryan staring at his feet. Me, staring at the "Happy New Year" sign and thinking, "We're already eighteen days into January. Time to take that shit down." The iodine injections. (Into. My. Nipples.) The child nurse who came to get me and then yelled at me for pulling down my mask.

And then me, all alone on a gurney, navigated into a room of strangers by a stranger (who just yelled at me about a fucking COVID mask).

Me alone with strangers is a common theme because this is how it is with ordeals of huge magnitude. Your ordeal is yours alone.

I was a mess of thoughts. There were decisions to be made and a million feelings to unpack. So, I did the only thing I knew to do—I started writing.

Because here's the truth. While you may be surrounded by family and friends and priests and neighbors, you *are* alone. You get wheeled into surgery alone. You close your eyes at night alone. You pray alone. There were times that I needed to be alone. But while I needed to be alone, I was also incredibly lonely.

I started having conversations with Candace. I don't know who Candace is. Is she the Ghost of Christmas Past? Is she a figment of my imagination? Is she an angel? I don't know. What I do know is that speaking to her openly, cussing her out, even writing letters to her helped. It helped me articulate my thoughts, my fears, and my loneliness.

I love the idea of writing letters, and I also love good dialogue. But when I started writing, I had no idea how cathartic it would become nor how much I needed it.

And now I've taken those letters and bound them together into one huge pile—a pile of emotions and questions, heartbreak and triumph, lessons and learnings. This is my book, built from my conversations with myself, my letters to no one, my rawest moments. It is my cancer in real time and my hard-fought restoration, spanning from January through May—from winter into spring, most literally.

But cancer is *my* ordeal of huge magnitude. Yours may be cancer, too. If so, welcome to the club no one wanted to join. Or you might be in the midst of a divorce, or drowning in debt, or trying to escape a cult. If you've picked up this book or been gifted it, then you are probably wading knee deep.

First, I'm sorry.

Whatever your ordeal of huge magnitude is, inevitably it is hard. It is painful, and it is raw. But it is also the beginning of the new you.

At the end of the day, ordeals of huge magnitude force us either to restore or to wither away. I chose restoration.

Restoration is a process. It takes time, patience, support, and a whole lot of kindness. Mostly to yourself. I also found it required a great deal of cussing.

Second, I'm rooting for you.

I don't know you or the personal struggles. But I do know we share a humanity that brings us together, even across the miles. Yes, even as strangers. My hope in writing this book is that you will find something in my experience that helps you. My ordeal was and still is a daily battle. I believe all ordeals are. They don't come and go; they aren't bookended with a clear beginning and end. They are often the result of a million little moments.

I also believe that stories unite. And that while my story isn't your story, there will be common threads to connect us. In fact, I firmly assert that if we just knew one another's stories rather than skin colors, ideologies, or identities, we'd realize what we have in common far outweighs that which we do not.

But fixing this world is a bit daunting…so let's just start here. With one another. Use my stories to help you articulate yours. And then, answer the question—so now what?

Because that's the point, right? I went through my restoration for a reason. You are too. You are going through this trial to get somewhere. You're fighting for a reason. And you have a say in your restoration. In fact, you have a say in everything. Use your voice. Tell your story. You are free to decide what comes next.

I wrote these entries in real time. But it would be silly to think your experience will mirror mine. It won't. Your ordeal of huge magnitude is yours alone. So go day by day or jump around. There are no rules. Except to be real and raw and honest. Cry at the snow, laugh at the absurdity of it all, and have a pity party. And then find your voice.

We were made to do hard things.

So now what?

Juli

Before we go any further, you should know that I love a properly placed cuss word.

My apologies in advance.

But I found cussing helps.

Feel free to get markers.
Use pens.
Or a pencil.
Color. Cuss. Write in rhyme.
Write letters. Write prose.
This is yours to do with what you will.

Books are made of paper, and paper is made to be written on.
So write. Sketch. Color. Doodle.
This isn't a library book…
Books have always been made to write in—not sure who ever said otherwise.
Must have been the original book banners.

Okay, friend.
From this point on, this is a no-judgment zone.
Only real conversations and raw emotions.
The only way to get to the other side is through.

Let's do this!

Feel free to use the blank pages along the way, or annotate in any open space. This is your canvas!

Table of Contents

Jump around, go day by day, no rules
Your OHM. Your story. Your voice.

Greet your pain.

This is new, but what do you have to say right now? Heads up, you're probably going to return to this again and again.

What is making you uncomfortable?

Who do you need to thank?

What conversations do you need to have with yourself?

What sacrifices are you making?

Making it through this day (I call this "crying at the snow").

What do you really need that you aren't saying?

Letting go…you know there is something that you have to let go, but it doesn't mean it's easy.

What have you overcome? (so far)

What keeps repeating?

What scares you?

What are mad about?

Have a pity party!

This is a marathon, not a sprint. What mile are you on?

Some solutions cost everything. What have you had to sacrifice?

Surviving is not the same thing as living.

What absurdities are you experiencing?

What are you being asked to analyze, examine, scrutinize?

Uncomfortable things.

When you stop and really listen, what do you hear?

Rock bottom.

Where do you see yourself in five years?

Who or what do you need to say goodbye to?

Not going to lie: Being a woman is really fucking hard.

The great before. That upper jab comes out of nowhere.

What have you found that you weren't looking for?

Wanna cuss someone out?

There are things we never thought we'd experience.

Surrendering.

What's happening in the world around you? It's still spinning.

It's almost spring. What are your angels saying?

Write your own prayer.

Strength. Resilience. Unconditional love = peace and hope to
do hard things.

Living is a choice. What do you choose today?

What would you exchange if you could?

How are you being restored?

Who is carrying your poop bag?

You're here now—no longer there.

What's your metaphor for the future?

It's easier to say "no," but you should say "yes."

What have you fucked up?

What do you really need to say?

Life has kept moving on around you…What needs to be said?

Father Time. He's an elusive SOB, isn't he?

Never, ever, ever, ever give up.

Call an asshole an asshole, or take a nap. This is your restoration.

Gifts come in the unlikeliest of places.

What do you miss?

Finding a new balance.

Glossary

Who's who, what's what, and the perfect word in the English language.

Fuck (verb, interjection, adjective, noun): You know the verb, but additionally, the word "fuck" can be used as an interjection (Fuck!) or an adjective (fucking cancer) or a noun (What the fuck?).

Candace: My cancer. She may very well be my intuition, my angel, or my nemesis. She's a bitch, but here to stay, and in the end, she gave me more than she took. It was just hard to see that at times.

Ryan, Cooper, Mackenzi (sometimes referred to as Doodle): My husband and children who would have loved to have not been included in this, but c'est la vie. Sometimes referred to as assholes.*

Doogie Howser: My plastic surgeon who is not actually a child but if I had found myself in a compromising situation in my teens, I could be his mother.

CJ: My cancer cat.

Scarlet: My Goldendoodle.

Ohio: Home. Both my original home and where I live now.

References to "teaching": I was a middle school teacher. I loved it. I also hated it. But I am unequivocally a better writer because of it.

Mary: Either my grandmother who is now one of my angels, or the OG Mary. I don't know, nor does it really matter. They are both pretty great.

53-year-old Trifecta: Semi-adult children, Alzheimer's, breast cancer.

Al: Alzheimer's, who is stealing my dad away bit by bit.

Substack: The software in which I wrote these letters. I joined Substack the fall before my diagnosis and it was going to be my writing "coming out" party place. Please join me there! *julibrenning.substack.com*

*If you know a mom that has never, ever referred to her children as assholes...don't trust her. She's a liar.

**If you're a mom and have never, ever referred to your children as assholes (at least silently), then you are an angel among us (or a liar).

While I obviously could have gone without having BC, I was so appreciative that it began in January. Lovely of the universe to provide me with such imagery.

January

"It's January and I'm kicking snow off the ground. I just threw out the flower you made me promise to water, handle with care, because I was too careless, you said. Careless with things and people, around me and behind and I remember being still for just a second or two, thinking that it's so much easier to leave and start anew, than take care of what's already here."

—Charlotte Eriksson

It is SO much easier to leave and start anew than to take care of what's already here but you can't. Emerging theme.

January 2

Hello Candace, my old friend.

I knew you'd find me, but your timing is always inexplicably bad.

Honestly though, December 22 seems to be an all-time low, even for you.

Alas, for Christmas this year, I got:

unexpected and fabulous time with my semi-grown children...

fleetingly precious time with my parents (and while Dad *is* fading, he's still the funniest one at the table)...

time with old friends and extended family, all of whom I adore...

...and breast cancer.

Just as I was coming to terms with my new friend AL (Alzheimer's), another uninvited guest has arrived.

So, Candace, a few things you should know before we begin our tête-à-tête:

I'm still getting over my anger and frustration at losing time to COVID-19, so I dare you to take any more of my time—you *will* be met with virulent passion and intensity.

You may get to hang out in my left boob (for now), but I am not letting you into my head (as much as possible) or my heart (ever).

You can have my boobs, my ovaries, *and* my fallopian tubes, but that's it.

You cannot stop me from making jokes, using the F-bomb whenever I choose, nor drinking wine. *(They won't make me stop drinking wine, will they? Bless the motherfuckers who suggest that as a treatment plan.)*

Welcome to the party, Candace.

May your stay be short, your conversation skills above par, and your party manners intact.

Here's to our new (hopefully very short) relationship,

Juli.

SO NOW WHAT?

Here you are…I'm sorry, but you may as well introduce yourself. The sooner you face it, the quicker you can get started. You can't get to the end without beginning. Greet your pain.

P.S. Welcome. I'm glad we're on this journey together.

January 3

Dear Candace,

The funny thing about being told you have cancer is the urgency.

Urgency for a diagnosis, urgency for answers, urgency for a plan, urgency to say what you haven't said and to plan what you haven't planned.

To live like you're dying.

—Which, I'm not. But I am. We all are. But now that I know I have cancer, I have a clue at the ending. When the fat lady is going to sing.

I'm not dying today, but today, I'm sad. Really, *really* sad. I'm sad and tired and anxious and mad and worried. So, so worried. What are my kids going to do? They are woefully ill-equipped to function without me. What in the fuck did I do wrong?

I used to take pride in my ability to be a mom. Kids like me. It's why I was a good teacher. My kids' friends like me, most of my students liked me— hell, *my own kids like me.* Most of the time.

I really thought I was good at the mom thing. You know, accepting and honest. They could have been gay or trans or Democrats or atheists…I didn't and do not care as long as they are happy, kind, functioning human beings.

As a mom, I am literally standing at the plate with two strikes at the top of the eighth inning.

Strike 1—the acquired one, so not technically mine to mother (although I did), has been arrested at least twice, and completely separated himself from us. Oh, and has a kid.

Strike 2—my brilliant (and I don't use that term lightly), hilarious, creative, athletic, competitive, compassionate son is living in our guest room with no earthly idea what to do with his life or college education.

Sitting dead-red, hoping to make contact with the third pitch—this one is showing potential. But for the love of all that's good, she's going to need to learn to make decisions on her own.

"I have cancer, kid. I can't help you decide if you feel like chicken or steak tonight. Godspeed."

Candace, I told you yesterday that you weren't allowed into my head. But alas, there you were from three to nine this morning.

Honestly, I've had better houseguests.

J.

SO NOW WHAT?

Shock and urgency. That's how ordeals of huge magnitude begin—with shock and then urgency. There are so many things you feel like you need to say and do…and right this minute. It's a lot easier to write it down than it is to lie awake in the middle of the night. So take some time now and write down what is shocking you and what urgent things you feel need to be done.

January 10

Oh dear Candace,

So. Yesterday was a lot.

I was beginning to not hate you, but then yesterday…

Ryan, Candace, and I met the plastic surgeon.

Doogie Howser was fine, nice, smart (even as he measured my boobs, talked about my nipples as if they were peel-and-stick stickers, and generally made me feel very, very old). He did his job so professionally.

He didn't mean to make me feel old, but he's a child.

And he was *measuring* my boobs.

The same boobs that I was so uncomfortable showing the world that I didn't even nurse my babies.

Those boobs.

Front and center. Photographed. The only topic of our discussion.

"Thank you, Candace, for literally forcing me to do exactly what makes me most uncomfortable."

The whole time we were in the room, Candace stood in the corner smirking.

Ryan kept his eyes anywhere other than on the twelve-year-old measuring my chest.

When I dressed and the young doctor and his very cute nurse gave us a minute, I asked Ryan, "Are you okay?"

To which he said, "This sucks."

Welcome to the party, love.

We got home just in time for me to take a walk with Scarlet (who isn't going to understand that we will soon have to take a hiatus) and Candace (who doesn't really know her place).

The air was cold and clean, and we walked for some time in silence. As the sun was shrinking, Candace said, "So, what's your plan? Oncoplasty plus five weeks of radiation, or mastectomy plus new boobs made of jellyfish?"

"Those options are as bad as Trump and Biden," I replied.

"And yet, they are all you get," she said with a sigh.

Indeed, my love, this sucks,

J.

SO NOW WHAT?

Decisions and doing exactly what makes you the most uncomfortable. That's the shit you get at the beginning: so many decisions to make. January 10 wasn't a great day. What is making you particularly uncomfortable today? What decisions are forcing you to stretch so far you might just split right in half? Write about it here—not necessarily to help you make any decisions, but just to get it all out there.

January 13

Dear Lovely, Large, Tattooed Lesbian,

Thank you for being so kind to me during that first mammogram. You are unknowingly my scarecrow, and I'm your Dorothy.

Your compassion and kindness set the tone of the journey. *To Oz we go!*

Dear Weirdly Energetic, Humanely Honest Radiologist,

Thank you for playing the 1980s Chillicothe High School soundtrack during my first long day of tests.

Nothing could make me feel more at home than a turkey baster in my boob to "Back in Black" and "Don't Stop Believin'."

Dear sweaty, itchy, menopausal armpits,

Thank you for hurting!

My apologies for neglecting you for so long. In fact, I've never given you (or my lymph nodes) a minute of my time. But! You, sweet things, just might have saved me. So.

Thank you. Truly.

Dear All of *You*,

Thank you for your words and your prayers and your positive energy.

I am going to keep writing about the hard stuff with humor when I can, and with honesty when I can't.

With love and appreciation,

Juli

Remember this and gift people you know who are struggling with a pack of thank-you notes it's a little gesture but perfect for when you want to help but don't know how. Honestly, how many fucking casseroles can people eat?

SO NOW WHAT?

I should have kept thank-you notes on hand and just written them as I moved about to all of the strangers being kind humans. Ordeals of huge magnitude are littered with kind strangers. It's pretty remarkable, but also really fucking easy to overlook. Today, thank one of those kind people—whether a stranger at a doctor's office, a family member, or even a body part. Write out your thank-you note below. If you're feeling up to it, snap a pic of the note and text it to them. Gratitude brings healing.

January 16

COFFEE WITH CANDACE

"So, you've decided?"

"The choices you've given me aren't great."

"I know. I'm sorry."

"You're sorry? Really?"

"I actually am sorry. It's hard being me."

"For fuck's sake, lady."

"Truly. I'm sure you can't see it now, it always takes time, but my job isn't to make you sick. I mean, it is, yes, but that is becoming increasingly harder with 3D imaging and badass women who insist on finding answers…so, I had to change my approach, rewrite the game. I used to be like Death's Amazon Driver. Now, I'm more of a teacher. It's a much nicer job description, but it's hard. Really hard."

"Teaching *is* hard."

"Indeed."

"But what are you trying to teach me? Just say it!"

"Oh. You know that's not how the best teachers do it. The best teaching comes quietly. You have to do it to learn it. Think of this as a group project that forces you to participate."

"I hate group projects."

"*Everyone does. Only educators believe that BS about working together, blah blah blah…but there is something to it.*"

"Like what?"

"*Like trusting other people. Releasing your own control. Playing your role while supporting others.*"

"I literally cannot roll my eyes high enough."

"*You know I'm right.*"

"Okay. Yes, you're sort of right, but…I just don't want to be here."

"*Nobody wants to be here.*"

"I know. I *do* know that."

"*So. What will it be?*"

"You mean, surgically?"

"*Yes. Decision #1…Will you follow your gut or the stats?*"

"My gut. I have to follow my gut. Health stats have never really been on my side."

"*Good.*"

"Really?"

"*Yes. Well done. You listened to you. You paid attention to you. You are taking care of you.*"

"So there really isn't a right or wrong?"

"*No.*"

"Fuck."

"Indeed."

"When are you moving on?"

"That depends on how well your group project goes and how long I'm needed."

"Kind of like Mary Poppins?"

"Yes. I suppose so."

"You're an ass."

"So, I've been told."

SO NOW WHAT?

I love dialogue! I used to teach an old Kurt Vonnegut story[1] that was just one long conversation. I love that story. What do you need to talk through with yourself? You probably should write it rather than have the conversation out loud or else someone might think you've lost it entirely.

1 | *A Long Walk to Forever*—totally worth a Google search!

January 18

COFFEE WITH CANDACE

"Okay, Candy. I've run my errands, gotten my gray colored, my toes done, even had a massage. I'm as ready as I am going to be…time for the coin toss?"

"No need. I'll defer."

"Wow. That's rich."

"I can be nice, you know."

"Right. I forgot. You're the misunderstood one. It's hard being Candace… yada yada…"

"It is."

"So you've said."

"How are you feeling? Really?"

"Are you my friend now?"

"No. Not exactly. But I've been with you for 648 hours (give or take). We have a 'bond,' as it were."

"Oh. That's what you're calling it? A bond? I suppose we do. However, I think of it more as a noose-rope relationship."

"Tom-a-to. To-mah-to."

"Words matter, Candace. My fucking life matters! I have things to do and no time for you."

"And yet…"

"And yet. Here you are. My noose."

"A bond."

"I am not going to discuss synonyms with you."

"Fine. All I really want to know is how you're doing. For real."

"I'm annoyed. I'm scared. I'm sad. But mostly, I'm determined."

"Good."

"Which part?"

"All of it, but mostly the determined part."

"Why?"

"Because you're going to need it. I'm sneaky. I'm a backhanded, conniving bitch who plays to win. Do you play to win?"

"Yes."

"Are you sure?"

"Yes. Mother F-er."

"Okay, then, my bonded friend: Game On."

"Game On."

SO NOW WHAT?

Mastectomy day. Sacrificial body part day. I hope your ordeal of huge magnitude didn't require a body part…but whatever is being asked of you, play hard. What sacrifices are you being asked to make? Document them. They may be necessary, but they should not go unnoticed.

January 23

Dear Candace,

Okay. Well. That was a thing.

Prior to surgery, I imagined you and I playing tennis or croquet—some kind of turn-of-the-century, *Downton Abbey* British yard game.

This is no fucking yard game.

In fact, thinking about it as a game at all implies a modicum of fun.

You may be having fun, but I assure you I am not.

This is a fight. A heavy weight *"Let's Get Ready to Rumble!!"* kind of fight.

A rumble is a dance between the *Sharks* and *Jets*, not a battle with combat weapons.

You came with combat weapons.

And, clearly, you've done this before. You had a battle plan. You waited patiently. You knew I'd break.

You probably thought it would be the moment I saw what was under the bandages. I admit, that was bad. And a moment that I would have preferred to have been drunk for.

But that wasn't it.

It wasn't even when my nerve endings woke up and I could literally *feel* the draining tubes sucking out what remained of my chest.

No. It was the snow.

It was watching the snow fall yesterday that broke me.

So, Candace, if you don't mind, I'm going to call a truce for a day or two and watch the snow fall.

Rest assured, I will be the one screaming, "*Adrienne!*" at the end of this fight. But I'm going to need a minute.

J.

SO NOW WHAT?

Cry at the snow. You're allowed. Okay, maybe you don't live where it snows. Cry at the rain. Cry at the bird perched on your backyard tree, building a nest for its little ones. There is beauty all around you, yet you are going through a living hell. But—and this cannot be emphasized enough—you woke up again today! It's okay, necessary even, to cry at the snow.

January 28

Dear Fellow Narcissists,

I am officially one week(ish) post-surgery. I have expanders for boobs, drains that hang like deflated testicles, and a declawed cat who won't leave my side.

On Wednesday, my childhood friend Debbie (a.k.a. Homecoming Queen currently morphing into a media mogul) hosted me as a guest on her podcast. And while I was not looking my best (I seem to think that sometimes I *do* look stage ready, but in reality…) it was a great experience. Primarily because she gave me the opportunity to speak *and* she asked one very profound question…

What have you found?

I should have seen that coming…the title of the show is *Find It!*, but my tête-à-tête with Candace didn't allow for interview prep.

I surprised myself when I answered, "My voice."

And this is true.

Sort of.

But mostly not.

In truth, I have *kind of* found my voice. Which is to say that I am just narcissistic enough to write letters into the ethers that are all about…(wait for it)…me!

This morning, I stumbled upon a new Substack: Black Snake of Vanity.

In his opening paragraph, he wrote, *Anyone who's a serious, driven writer is, in my opinion, to some extent great or small of the "narcissistic variety."*

Thank you, Kind Sir, for that justification.

Because all of a sudden, that's me: Queen Narcissist and her friend, Candace.

This is hard shit. The hardest thing I've ever done. And I'm not even dying. I just have cancer.

I have cancer.

I can name her. I can cuss her out and cut her out. But I still have cancer.

I don't think that sentence will ever be written in the past tense.

And I don't think it should. It's a part of me now. It's a "sliver of who I am" (thank you, Kind Sir, for that phrase too).

After Wednesday, many wrote and called me "brave."

I am not brave. Let's be clear.

I'm just alone and all wrapped up in me.

And I *need* to be alone in this. Because (and this is the other thing I said Wednesday that I didn't even know I was thinking) I was the only one wheeled into that operating room.

Those boobs that were sliced off have only ever been mine. This is only *really* happening to me.

My conversations with Candace are the only honest conversations I'm currently having.

So, thank you for your kindness, but I'm not brave.

IF.

I had fully found my voice and was brave…

…when people ask, "What do you need?"

…I would say:

I need you to sit with me.

I need to cry.

I need to laugh.

I need you to cry and laugh *with* me.

I need you to tell me you're scared too.

I need you to join my pity party.

I need to *know* that my children and Ryan will be okay.

I need to trust.

I need to have faith.

I need to believe.

I need you to hear me.

I need you to read what I write.

I need you to think I'm funny.

I need to get these fucking drains out.

But for now, I need to be alone.

My best,

J.

Why is asking for what we need so hard?

SO NOW WHAT?

What do you need? I mean really **need**. *Find your voice. Some good things have to come from this or what's it all for anyway? Write those needs right here. The next time someone asks you how they can help, remember this list and consider sharing one or two items with that person who cares for you. A burden shared is a burden lighter.*

January 30

Dear Diary,

Last night, as I closed my eyes, I thought back to the other time I was put to bed.

That was twenty-three years ago.

Mackenzi was eager to make her debut, but it wasn't time…bedrest for five weeks.

It was Ryan, Coop, and me.

Then and Now.

It was hard to be still and let Ryan do all the heavy lifting. And Coop— just two and a half—had no way of understanding. But each night, he'd crawl in bed with me, and we'd watch a movie. *(There's less cuddling now, but we still watch movies.)*

Cooper hated going to sleep alone. We tried everything. A dog. An aquarium. Music. Books. *So many books*. But he just didn't like the closing-his-eyes-alone part. Still doesn't.

One night late in the fourth week, Ryan put Coop to bed and then joined a friend for a walk. I was downstairs.

Sometime later, I was on the couch and Coop was at the top of the stairs.

Just one wall, twenty-seven stairs, and an ocean between us.

"Mommy?"

"Yes, sweet boy, are you okay?"

"I'm scared. I'm all alone."

"Do you have Key?"

"Yes."

"Are Key and Petey with you?"

"I have Key. Petey is here."

"Then you're not alone. Can you take Key and climb back in bed? Petey will go with you. Daddy will be home soon."

"I need you."

"I know, but I can't come to you right now."

"I'm sad."

"Me too."

"I'm going to sleep right here with Petey and Key."

"Okay. I'm sorry."

"Mommy, I'm scared."

"So am I, Coop. So am I."

"Can you sing the baseball song?"

"Yes. I can sing the baseball song."

So I sang the baseball song.

Soon, his cries slowed, then stopped.

My tears were fast and furious as I realized that I would never be able to take all his fears away, nor really do anything more than sing him to sleep.

When Ryan came home, he found me all cried out. And at the top of the stairs, behind the baby gate we'd placed for precisely this, he found a little boy and a golden retriever, curled up together with a disintegrating blankie named "Key."

I hadn't relived that memory in years.

But yesterday, as Ryan and Cooper—now *twenty-five* and a half—"discussed" Cooper's next steps, I thought of that night.

Twenty-three years later. Again I am a wall, twenty-seven stairs, and an ocean away…

Juli.

P.S. I know you're trying to teach me things, Candace, but I'm not a fan right now.

SO NOW WHAT?

I had so many lessons to learn. So many fucking lessons and so much letting go. Letting go is a critical part of enduring an ordeal of huge magnitude that most are not prepared for. We understand the "fight" command, but the "letting go" seems to be counterintuitive. But there is so much—too much—that cannot be controlled. Channel your inner Elsa and "Let it go!"

January 31

COFFEE WITH CANDACE

"So, Candace, what do you have up your sleeve? What's next?"

"Silly you. You know I can't show my hand this early. Besides, I love surprises."

"I don't."

"Funny that you still think you have control over this narrative."

"I do. Sort of."

"Yes. Sort of. You get to determine how you react. You get to determine how you fight, which determines the direction the next chapter takes."

"Kind of like those old *Encyclopedia Brown* mysteries."

"Kind of."

"I'm not sure how to begin."

"Begin what?"

"Living, I guess. I mean, I've been 'living,' but living in a room by myself. Like some kind of surreal, weird, book-filled purgatory. Half-ass living."

"It's winter. It's fine."

"Good point. But."

"But what?"

"I'm not dead. I'm supposed to do something about this not-dead thing."

"Give it time…It's winter. Read. Rest. Heal. Wait patiently for the next surprise. I assure you, I'm very good at this game."

"It's not a game."

"Oh right. It's a fight. Float like a butterfly, sting like a bee. I'm good at that too. Actually, I'm great at that. I'm the real deal. So rest up, my friend…it's not a fair fight if you're not at your best…and where would the fun be in that?"

"You're an ass."

"So you've said."

"And, arrogant."

"Indeed."

SO NOW WHAT?

January was hard. Physically and emotionally. Beginnings sort of suck. Think back to your beginning. Maybe it's been a month. Maybe your "beginning" has taken almost a year. But no matter how long it's been, you've made it this far. What have you overcome to get here?

February

"The day and time itself: late afternoon in early February,
was there a moment of the year better suited for despair?" [2]

—*Alice McDermott*

2| Amen!

February 2

Dear Candace,

A friend just said to me, "you know we're supposed to learn lessons from tragedy."[3]

Maybe that's why Shakespeare wrote so many tragedies. While the comedies teach us to laugh at our foibles, the tragedies make us look in the mirror.

So, thanks, Candace, for that.

It wasn't my intention to spend January looking in the mirror. But alas,

This is what I've learned:

1. I'm a master over-stepper. This seems to be my superpower.

2. Clearly, my family is incapable of speaking to one another without me as an interpreter.

3. Also just as clearly, I am wildly narcissistic.

4. And while I appreciate the clarity not drinking wine affords, I miss it.

5. But sitting on a bed, staring out a window...sober...only amplifies numbers 1–4.

3| Same friend who coined the phrase "Ordeal of Huge Magnitude"!

FFS, Candy, I get it. I obviously have shit to figure out.

However, your repetition is superfluous *and* unnecessary.

Here's to February,

J.

SO NOW WHAT?

When my students were struggling to figure out what point an author was trying to make, I'd tell them to find the repetition. Candace's repetition was superfluous but not unnecessary. There are still lessons I am learning. Most of them are really fucking hard. What is playing on repeat?

February 6

COFFEE WITH CANDACE

"You've been quiet."

"Thanks for noticing…but you have kind of usurped my thoughts. "

"Usurp? That's quite a violent word. I prefer the word 'consume.'"

"Again, you and synonyms. I'm not interested in debating connotations."

"But the right word changes everything! You of all people know that, but truly it's neither here nor there whether you think of the occupation of your thoughts as usurpation or consumption. I've pitched my tent. I have all the time in the world. So…pray tell…what's rattling around in there? Why so quiet?"

"Actually, this morning, I read this quote, '…and what's the use of talking, if you already know that others don't feel what you feel?' That's how I feel, Candace. That."

"Well that's rather assumptive of you."

"Experience leads to belief."

"That it does. But you are mistaken if you believe that I've only 'usurped' your thoughts. I am a 'house' guest, after all. And none of you have any experience with me."

"Exactly!"

"Then what is the problem? I have given you a lot to think about, a lot to work on, a lot to talk about. I'm doing my part. Time for you to stop feeling sorry

for yourself and do yours."

"Wow. You are such an ass."

"So you've said…and yet…"

"And yet."

"Okay, so maybe I should have asked 'what are you scared of?'"

"Thank you."

"That, my friend, is the first time you've thanked me."

"You're not my friend. But thanks for asking…That's all I needed. Some-one to ask me what I'm scared of."

"Well?"

"I'm not ready to say that out loud. Yet. And, honestly, I don't know how to start."

"Take your time. The first chapter is always the hardest to write. And appar-ently, I'm not leaving any time soon."

"Indeed."

SO NOW WHAT?

What scares you? Identifying it is the first step in facing it. And facing it is the only way to survive. Even if you aren't ready to say your fears out loud, write them here. Sketch them.

February 10

Dear Diary,

I'm still not taking calls.

And, yes, I get that makes me a fucking princess. But. I just can't talk.

I *talked* to my new physical therapist yesterday. That was enough.

While I'm not talking a lot, I *am* doing a lot of reading and thinking.

When I envisioned recovery, I had images of peacefully quiet moments of meditation.

So…it's not that.

In reality, it's a lot of angst. Angst about my future. About what I'm writing. About who is reading what I'm writing. About becoming self-absorbed. About being mad.

I'm mad. *(Yesterday, Vanessa, my PT, told me it's okay to be mad.)*

I'm mad about cancer. I'm mad about Alzheimer's. I'm mad about the pandemic. I'm mad at the narrative.

I'm mad at the verbose elitists of the world. I'm mad that I have square inserts sewn into my chest which were clearly designed by a man.

And, this is the thing…

I really didn't want to write about cancer. I wanted to make people laugh, peer out from a slightly different lens, ponder…

But here I am mostly writing about cancer.

And being mad.

And since I'm pretty sure that conversation is getting old, let me fill you in on what I've been reading and watching and thinking about during my down time:

I read about the Cochrane report. Have you read this? Probably not because mainstream media hasn't published it. It doesn't fit the narrative.

I reread the *Tao of Pooh* because I have nothing but time. It's still fabulous. And made me think that Alzheimer's is a lot like Taoism or at least Pooh. And that made me feel a tad better *(about my dad, not our president).*

And then I pulled out my copy of *Animal Farm* because, let's be honest, it hits awfully close to home.

And then I watched *The Last of Us*. It's brilliant and terrifying. This *could* be us. We could literally be living in a fucking game. With floating spy balloons.

And then one day this week, I thought, *I will reach out to another writer on Substack and asked for a recommendation. ("Advice" from the Powers That Be.)*

She told me "No."

Which is fine. Of course. I get it.

I *am* quite self-absorbed right now and *may not* be seeing the world clearly, but I just don't understand why people are so leery of helping each other?

The world is obviously coming to an end soon…There are unknown balloons counting livestock over Montana…help a sister out!

That all brings me back to Substack, which I'm reading a lot of…

I love the new ideas, the things I'm learning. Just in the last two days, I have read essays about transgender surgery, Tarot cards, mascara, the Memphis police, spy balloons, masks, God, paganism, and Andrew Tate. Who, apparently, was the most Googled person of 2022. Who knew? Actually, millions, just not me.

The Free Press.

It's all good shit.

But.

There is a lot of arrogance in this world. And writers are the worst. And while Substack claims to be a new, freeing place (which it is!), it's also an old-school club of verbose elitists. You know who got a shout-out yesterday from Substack? Kareem Abdul-Jabbar!

Pretty sure Kareem didn't need a helping hand.

I have 458 subscribers. And I appreciate every single one.

In actuality, only 455 people read *Dear John*, because three are my little family, and they

don't. But it's okay. If they did, they'd realize how often I write about them.

But. Out of the 455, none are famous or *New York Times* columnists or NBA basketball stars. They are regular everyday people who have no control over the Twitter algorithm; who are appalled that our political debates are between dumb and dumber; who are actually trying to teach children or raise children who have been f-ed up from the world's reaction to a virus; who have cancer and have to pay taxes and don't qualify for student loan forgiveness; who don't have time to read nineteen-minute diatribes because, well, life; who aren't confused about their gender but feel for those who are; who are from wildly normal places like Ohio and Tennessee; and who are just everyday humans.

Taking nothing away from Kareem, but this is *my* shout-out to everyone else.

Power to the People!

Still don't care!

And since it's national news that Aaron Rodgers is going into the dark for four days, I guess it's okay that I'm just sitting here in Ohio, mad. Here's to us both finding the light.

And me not being so mad. Which I'm learning is just a side effect of my relationship with Candace.

J.

SO NOW WHAT?

So mad. So, so mad. When I wasn't sad, that is. What are you mad about? I'm no expert, but it's probably okay if you're mad. I still get mad some days. What makes you so mad you would spit if adults could go around spitting in polite society?

February 14

"Crying is boring and feeling sorry for yourself is ugly."

—Alex Dimitrov, poet extraordinaire

SO NOW WHAT?

So much for Valentine's Day. Who are you going to invite to your pity party?

February 15

Dear Candace,

> *"At mile 20, I thought I was dead. At mile 22, I wished I*
> *was dead. At mile 24, I knew I was dead. At mile 26.2, I*
> *realized I had become too tough to kill."*

Not going to lie. This "relationship" of ours is not for the faint of heart.

Right now, this tête-à-tête feels less like a lovely conversation and more like a marathon.

I started strong…but this week felt like mile 22. Maybe 24.

- Week One: Woo-hoo. I'm alive! I don't have boobs, but…you can't have it all.

- Week Two: I got this! Sleeping in, coffee in bed, princess living is not so bad.

- Week Three: I literally can not feel a positive emotion. Fuck off.

- Week Four: We'll see.

I'm no runner, but I recognize that you are quite, quite good.

Just when I was physically beginning to take the lead, you fought back with psychological warfare.

Well played, Candass.

Very well played.

J.

SO NOW WHAT?

It's a fucking marathon. You're too tough to kill, but that doesn't mean it's easy. OHMs don't come with a timeline, and none of them are a sprint. What mile are you on? How are you going to get to the finish line?

February 16

Dear You,

DEI aside,[4]

Let's be honest about who is "qualified" for particular jobs.

While I want to live in a world where everyone is *exactly* like everyone else. We don't.

And some things simply cannot be understood by men.

Case in point, tissue expanders post-mastectomy.

First, I feel like this should go without saying but…

Boobs are not square.

Clearly, as a society we have *not* insisted that tissue expanders be designed by women. Moreover, we have allowed men to write explanations on our world wide web.

For example, a simple Google search provides the following:

> *Most of the discomfort occurs during your tissue expansion appointments. Our surgeons will inject saline into your tissue expanders over the course of several months to stretch the surrounding tissues. This can be unpleasant because it puts pressure on your muscles.*

4| Diversity, equity, and inclusion.

While I have no proof that a man wrote this, there are a couple of clues.

> *"Most of the discomfort occurs during your tissue expansion appointments."*

Uh. No.

There is a ton of pain prior to actual expansion, and the word "discomfort" connotes a slight skin abrasion.

And unpleasant?

Unpleasant is a gray day in the low sixties…

Filling a chest cavity with saline on top of square tissue expanders is not a gray day in the low sixties nor a slight skin abrasion.

If a woman wrote that definition it would read:

> *While it absolutely sucks that you had to have your boobs removed to save your life, medical advancements are the real thing. However, the field of tissue expander design still has an impenetrable glass ceiling and remains a country-club, good-ole-boy network. Therefore, the expanders that will be placed after mastectomy are square and plastic. They are miserable and very painful. But rest assured, that doesn't compare to the pain of filling said expanders with saline. That will bring you to your knees and be akin to shoving needles under your fingernails. But. You will survive it. For you are the sex that endures a monthly outpouring of blood, hot flashes, mood swings, unexplained weight gain, and childbirth. You got this.*

To be fair, a woman probably isn't qualified to design a prosthetic penis—at least from a comfort standpoint—so, in that, we *are* equal.

Equality for all!

And yes, good gentleman doctors of the world, hot flashes, weight gain, and joint pain *will* affect my quality of life. Let us please stop sugarcoating hormone fluctuations.

But. Alive, I will be.

Juli

And for those of you going through BC, keep fighting the good fight. Some of the treatments are not for the faint of heart!

SO NOW WHAT?

Boobs aren't square. And sometimes the solution to a problem is almost as painful as the problem, and that's pretty much bull-shit. But…c'est la vie. What solutions have you had to endure lately that are just plain painful?

February 17

Dear Diary,

I had several people reach out to me after Wednesday's post asking if tissue expanders are actually square. Doogie Howser says they aren't square, but they do have sharp edges. I think Doogie might be splitting hairs, and I'm no geometrist (potential new job for Coop?) but sharp edges mean square to me.

My apologies for only two posts this week.

Full transparency: I may have painted myself into a corner with this letter-writing thing.

Some days, I don't have a letter to write, nor am I very witty, but it does save you from enduring the other nonsense I'm writing. In fact, this week, I wrote an "essay" about COVID, cancer, Alzheimer's, and death. That's some funny shit right there.

You're welcome.

Ryan says that I need to write a note saying how great my doctors are. He also mentioned that I sound, at times, a little negative, and sort of like a man-hater. Who knew he reads these silly missives?

Sorry for the negativity. I blame it on cancer.

Man-hater?

I like men. I just feel like if you're going to talk about hormonal fluctuations, then you should have to experience them for yourself. That's all.

However, I *will* say my team of doctors are rock stars.

It's been a tough week for the Buckeye state with train wrecks and toxic spills, while experiencing three of the four seasons, but it *is* a great place to have cancer.

This week's takeaways:

- Week 4 was better than Week 3.

- Sports reporters are idiots.

- Is a potentially pregnant Rihanna really national news?

- Funny that there is a database of research updated in real time regarding breast cancer and yet not for things like worldwide viruses. That's curious.

- Figuring out how to live again is not for sissies.

- Surviving is not the same thing as being alive.

- I want to be friends with Nellie Bowles.

- In addition to new boobs, I want a tattoo, and I don't mean nipples.

Cheers, friends.

May your weekend be filled with whatever season is appropriate for your corner of the world in February—no toxic spills and good Chianti.

And a very happy birthday to the presidents.

Juli

SO NOW WHAT?

Surviving is not *the same thing as living. Don't let anyone tell you otherwise, but how are you going to live now? Now that things are forever changed?*

February 18

Dear Weekenders,

I noticed that more people read these short, little missives on the weekend. Not sure what that says about you or me. But I don't really care.

(I would like to give a shout-out to my daughter, who not only read yesterday's letter but corrected my spelling. Bless you, child.)

While the majority of the Substack newsletters I'm reading are loooong (but well written), I maintain there's power in brevity. I also realize that cancer has given me nothing but time. However, you (the living) are busy. So I thank you for stopping your busy lives to read.

I will continue to try and say more with less.

Speaking of small talk…

While filling my boobs, well-intentioned Doogie Howser tried to have a conversation.

I'm not a master small talker normally, but lying on my back while having saline injected into what used to be a body part only seen by few is a bit of a challenge.

This is how our conversation went:

"So, done anything interesting lately?"

"Other than cancer. Not really."

"Gone on any trips?"

"Your timeline has me a little homebound."

"Yes, I guess it does. Any questions?"

And that's how our conversations always end. Any questions?

Wonder what he'd do if I said yes, as a matter of fact...

- What was the ugliest pair of boobs you've ever seen?

- Have you ever been asked to do a size G? H?

- Was your mother concerned with this obsession as a young boy?

Maybe next week, I will go to the appointment prepared with a game of *Would You Rather?*

- "So, Doogie, would you rather create small, perky boobs or large, bouncy ones?"

- "Would you rather remove or rebuild body parts?"

- "Would you rather do 'research' on a topless beach in the south of France or Brazil?"

According to his timeline, I'm going to be having these clandestine meetings for the next five weeks.

I fear we may have already reached a conversational threshold, so please feel free to submit questions for Doogie below.

Juli

SO NOW WHAT?

There is absurdity in every ordeal of huge magnitude. It's just sometimes hard to find it. The absurdity of my breast cancer was the conversations I had while having saline injected into my boobs. Find the absurd. It's there somewhere. And while you're looking for the absurd, feel free to continue to say "Fuck off." Just because there are absurdities doesn't mean this doesn't suck.[5]

5 | And if you want, send me some absurdities! I want to laugh through tears alongside you... julibrenning.com.

February 21

Dear Candace,

> *As I am writing this…I am on hold with a pharmaceutical
> company. I have been subjected to the same three refrains of
> music for an hour and forty-seven minutes (so far).*

> *This is living with cancer in real time…*

Yesterday, my friend referred to you, Candace, as my "ordeal of huge
magnitude."

That is exactly what you are! My oohm. My *om.*

*(And just like
that a title is born!)*

And that made me think of yoga.

Honestly, this relationship of ours *is* beginning to feel like a very long, very
bad yoga class. And I say that as a yogi.

And as any yogi will tell you, when it's done right—when the body, mind,
and spirit mingle and mix all together—yoga can be hard as hell.

Since I'm on hold (still), I looked up the meaning of "om."

This is literally the first thing that I uncovered. Can't make this shit up.

> *In the Hindu tradition, the sound of om is said to contain
> the entire universe. It is the first sound from the beginning of
> time, and it also encompasses the present and the future. As
> such, its importance and power are difficult to overstate. In*

the chakra system, it is connected to Ajna chakra, the third eye, which represents intuition and self-knowledge.

Thank you, Candace, my *om*, for forcing me to examine my present and analyze my future. For coercing me to probe into my intuition and scrutinize my self-knowledge.

Your power *is* difficult to overstate.

But I suppose that is precisely what ordeals of huge magnitudes are for— examining, analyzing, probing, and scrutinizing.

So…

With appreciation?

J

SO NOW WHAT?

Examining? Analyzing? Probing? Scrutinizing? OHMs ask a lot of you. Dig as deep as you want…Some things are better for our subconscious to unpack. But what are you discovering that you'd rather not?

February 25

Dear Candace,

Today's appointment with Doogie was as uncomfortable as the last.

Funny thing about diving into the world of BC: You discover it's not uncommon for women to have a photo shoot. *(Kudos to those women!)*

Since I'm not one of the new-boob BC-ers who have boudoir photos taken, I will have to try and paint this picture with words.

First, you have to envision the space. Today's appointment took place in a satellite office which is literally in a mall. A nice, high-end mall. But a mall.

And it's a spa. For women with frankly too much money.

Everyone at the spa today were lovely humans. Frozen, botoxed, sad-behind-the-eyes humans. But lovely.

And me.

Unshowered. Because why?

I *should* have showered because I smell. It's not my fault. My hormones are literally raging war against me and have decided that the best tactical move is hourly extreme temperature fluctuations.

It was a real-life game of *one of these things is not like the other.*

There was a palpable sigh of relief (from everyone) when I was taken into the room.

The room was pristine, clean, and modern with kind lighting.

This was my first solo visit. So. Just me.

I sat center stage on the princess throne hospital table.

At a slight, comfortable recline.

Bare-chested.

Square/rhomboid boobs fully exposed, east-to-west scars across said *Frankenstein*-ian creations.

Doogie on one side, injecting saline.

Perfectly sculpted child nurse on the other side, injecting saline.

And the three of us had a lovely conversation.

In the corner, Candace stood giggling. Overjoyed at the absurdity and discomfort she has provided me.

F you, Candace.

Juli

SO NOW WHAT?

I had to face so many things that made me feel uncomfortable. I used to tell my husband that every day offered me a new opportunity to do precisely what I hated most. What is making you uncomfortable?

February 28

Dear February,

You were a lot.

I had wild imaginings about the healing process. I was sure I would be up and about (physically and emotionally) in a couple of weeks. They said six to eight.

I didn't believe them.

They were right.

Listen with your eyes.

That's the phrase on repeat in my head. *Listen with your eyes.* Guess that's my new mantra. My March mantra. *Listen with your eyes.*

Since January 1, I've been writing every day—365 days with Candace—and it's remarkable (and hard) to return to the *then*.

It's easy to look back and see things differently. Looking back is not nearly as honest as seeing in real time. Real time is much rawer. Not sure that's a word. Raw, Rawer, Rawest? I don't care. I like it.

Rawer.

I wrote this in real time on February 11.

February, dear February, you are a bitch

You claim to be the month of love and presidents and groundhogs

But really,

You're cold. And windy. And gray.

You're always in second place.

Always the bridesmaid,

And I used to like you.

This year, not so much.

I'm a March girl.

So please, please, please, Candace.

I will give you February

Just don't take my March.

I don't claim to be a poet, but, February, you *were* cold and windy and gray.

Be gone, #2, I've got some listening to see,

Juli

I think listening requires all five senses.

SO NOW WHAT?

I'm no poet. But try it. You might surprise yourself. February was cold and windy and gray. Literally and metaphorically. But I got through it. Officially two months in. When you stop and listen. Really listen. What do you hear? And see?

March

"Yes, but it's, you know—every year, you're all, 'March! This is going to be great! Start of spring!' But it's definitely not, right? Because there will be a weird, freak snowstorm, and it's like winter's started all over. Unexpected things happen in March."

—*Kate Clayborn*[6]

March

6| Yes, Kate Clayborn! Yes, fucking fabulous frivolous March! (I don't know Kate but would like to.)

March 2

Dear Rock Bottom,

I heard J.K. Rowling say, "Rock bottom became the solid foundation on which I rebuilt my life."

That gave me a little hope because if she can acknowledge the power of rock bottom, then so can I.

Landing on rock bottom is not nearly as difficult as sinking. The sinking is the hard part.

You can watch yourself sink deeper and deeper while every decision you make adds weight to the block of cement tied to your ankle…

You are sinking.

And sinking.

Until eventually you hit the bottom of the pond. And only on the solid foundation of the bottom can you untie that cement block and free yourself.

Then you can push off.

And hopefully make it to the surface.

The other night, Coop said to me, "I'm at rock bottom, Mom." And at first, I was so sad, but then I thought, "Thank God." *Finally, he can start swimming.*

The last few weeks, Candace definitely forced me to vacillate between treading water and sinking. There has been no swimming. But this week, I finally hit the bottom. I hope.

Like Coop, now I can start swimming.

So, thank you, Rock Bottom, for being solid ground, and for being a constant in all our lives. You rarely get the credit you deserve.

Yours truly,

Juli

SO NOW WHAT?

Treading water is fine. And sinking sucks. But from the bottom at least you can push off. Have you hit rock bottom? (You might sink back down. It's okay. The nice thing about the bottom is that it's always there.)

March 3

COFFEE WITH CANDACE

"Happy Birthday."

"Thank you. Although it would be happier if you weren't here. Or if I had estrogen. And wine."

"You can have wine. Just in moderation."

"Right. Moderation."

"Moderation is a good thing. And besides, you needed me."

"No, I didn't."

"Yes. You did. You needed a reset. So, you're welcome."

"I didn't thank you for that. I thanked you for wishing me a happy birthday."

"Semantics, my friend. It's all just semantics, and perspective. Perspective is everything. Look how far you've come! You shower most days. You've gone to the grocery store, tried your hand at glassblowing, gone out to dinner, and even worn real clothing. It's a brand-new set of days. It's your new year. So what is it you want for your birthday?"

"Estrogen."

"Besides that. Estrogen is my weapon of choice, you can *have it, but then I have a decided advantage."*

"World peace? Someone other than Trump or Biden to seek office? A way to change the volume on Alexa without getting up? Sugar bags that don't spill? A *NYT* bestseller?"

"How about 365 more days?"

"I'll take that."

"Then 365 more. Plus 365 plus 365 plus 365."

"How many is that? I don't do math."

"That's 1,825. It's not guaranteed that you will get all 1,825. But the odds are in your favor for five more years. At least from my perspective."

"Five years."

"Indeed. You fought for this. You gave your boobs for this. So what will do with them…these 1,825 days?"

"Not sure. But something forward."

"Yes. To quote your Dad, "I suggest you go forward."

"Candace, thank you."

"Oh, friend. No need to thank me. You won this round fair and square. Now it's up to you to do something with your winnings."

"We aren't friends."

"So you've said."

SO NOW WHAT?

Five years is a cancer thing. "We can keep you alive for five years, then five more. Anything after that is gravy. Woo-hoo!" Depending on what OHM you are battling, your threshold may be much longer…or even much shorter. But pretend you get just five years. What are you going to do with them?

My dad is one of my favorite humans. I love being his daughter. But bearing witness to his painfully slow decline is heart-wrenching. Cancer is a formidable opponent, but Alzheimer's is a whole other level of hell. It is like watching him sail to the land of elsewhere inch by inch. One thing I'm trying to do is remember his stories. In his prime, he was a master storyteller. Funny. Just inappropriate enough. Succinct. And often the lessons he taught us came in story form, and later morphed into stories of their own.

One of my favorites goes like this:

> *I was a senior in college. The youngest of three, therefore, my graduation marked a significant pay raise. I had an old two-toned brown Toyota Camry which had a tendency to wreck. Often. One spring day, I hopped into my old two-toned brown Camry to discover that I had no reverse, which seems like a little thing until you stop and think about the necessity of backing up.*
>
> *I called him (from a landline—1992) fully assuming he would send me to the mechanic whom I now knew personally.*
>
> *After listening intently about the injustices of driving a car (that he paid for) without reverse, he simply and emphatically said, "Well, Jules, I suggest you go forward."*

I drove that car only forward for three months.

March 6

Dear "December 22nd Me,"

Some things happen in life that change everything.

I will never forget sitting in a bathtub after Cooper was born. Crying. Mourning my old self.

It doesn't really matter how you become a mother. Whether you adopt, acquire, give birth…once you're a mom, you are never not a mom.

And while I was thrilled, I was also sad that my pre-mom life was over.

Mourning is a real thing.

> *I mourn my dad as Alzheimer's peels him away.*
>
> *I mourn my life before children.*
>
> *I mourn my life before adulthood.*
>
> *I mourn my life before grown children.*
>
> *I mourn my life before cancer.*

My emotions have been messy, messy, messy since my diagnosis. Some days I am nothing but hopeful; others I'm pissed off; others I'm on top of the world; and others I'm sad.

All days I'm overwhelmed.

My heart is literally overflowing.

My oldest friends stopped their lives to celebrate my birthday, and yesterday I could barely get out of bed 1) because we stayed up too late and the beer was ice cold, 2) because these stupid expanders were not made for deep belly laughs, and 3) because this we share—our mourning and our celebrations—and it took all of me.

I didn't know that I needed them as much as I did.

I'm not too proud to say I need other women in my life. Women who can mourn and celebrate simultaneously.

Because I now understand that one does not exist without the other.

I cannot be on this side of cancer without a diagnosis.

Just like I cannot know the hardships and joys of motherhood without being a mom.

But. Mourning is real. And okay. Maybe even necessary.

And laughter through tears *is* the finest of emotions. Thank you, friends, for both.

So, December 22nd Me, thank you for the 52+ years before cancer. I miss you, but also say goodbye.

Juli.

SO NOW WHAT?

That person you were before your OHM is gone. You will never be that person again. This is the new you. And while you may not be all the way through the tunnel, you're making progress. Write your goodbye letter.

March 10

Dear Women,

The other day, Coop said, "Mom, I think we've reached the threshold of conversations involving your boobs."

I love a predominately silent, funny human who speaks only when necessary.

Say less, everyone!

It's been a long week of appointments and a lot of discussion about my boobs.

I don't love boobs. Never have. Didn't nurse my babies because…gross.

I incubated them for nine months, taught them to read, gave them passports, sent them to college, gave them books and guitars and cleats…feeding them from my body was never on my parenting radar.

And now here we are all these years later, talking about my boobs. (Oh how I wish I had gotten cancer of the elbow.)

Thinking about my boobs made me think about being a woman. And thinking about being a woman made me think about all the unhappiness involving gender.

To quote Nellie Bowles of The Free Press (who I desperately want to be friends with), there is no place for those of us who land in the middle.

It's no man's land.

I firmly stand in the middle of the road when it comes to gender. I support and empathize with anyone who struggles with gender identity (I truly can't imagine) and yet I have no good answers when it comes to things like gender-specific sports.

But this, I think: If a naturally born genetically specific male (did I say that correctly?) feels like they should have been born a female, then, it's only fair to insist that they know exactly what they are signing up for.

Obviously, this is not an extensive list, but for starters:

- A monthly shedding of internal cells.

- Bloating for no apparent reason.

- Bras that literally contain metal.

- Night sweats.

- Underwear that is twice as expensive and will inevitably be ruined.

- An influx of estrogen, depletion of estrogen, influx, depletion, influx, depletion repeatedly from age twelve until the end of time.

- Episiotomies. (If you don't know, look it up.)

- A forced pregnancy that you may or may not have the right to do anything about.

- And the icing on the cake: yeast infections.

If you still want to be a woman after all of that, then welcome to the club!

March

It is not for the faint of heart.

May your weekend be blood-free, hormonally balanced, and most importantly, your wine expensive and perfectly chilled.

Juli

March

SO NOW WHAT?

Being a woman is hard. It just is. You might not be a woman, but odds are if you're relating to my story this much, you are. It's okay to acknowledge that some things are simply horseshit. But what are you going to do about it?

March 14

Dear Candace,

I gotta hand it to you…just when I was starting to get arrogantly proud of myself, you came back with an uppercut and then a left jab.

Last week, I met with my doctors, made a plan, picked out my implants (which *should* have been fun but you aren't fun…)

And then treatment began.

Oh my word.

FFS, Candy, I gave you a body part!

In the whole scheme of things, that should have evened the score…but no. Now you demand all of my hormones.

Which is fine.

Who needs to sleep anyway?

Or have access to all of their mental capabilities?

And sweating through sheets is sexy as hell. Ask anyone.

I mean, who am I to complain? I'm alive. For five to ten more years.

But this is the thing, Candass. I wasn't sick.

At Thanksgiving, I wasn't sick.

At Christmas, I wasn't sick.

Both of the days the Buckeyes broke my heart, I wasn't sick.

But now. Now I'm sick.

Fuck you,

J.

March

SO NOW WHAT?

Oh, the great "Before." That upper jab comes out of nowhere, doesn't it?

What hit you the hardest?

March 16

Dear A.A. Milne,

I don't *have* cancer.

I *had* cancer.

I removed it. I offered my boobs to the cancer gods, and they accepted them.

I *had* a tumor that came unannounced, uninvited, and with a vengeance.

It's gone.

But presently,

I *have* two children trying desperately to launch, no estrogen, and a dad with Alzheimer's.

The 53-year-old trifecta!

> *"I think it's more to the right," said Piglet nervously. "What do you think, Pooh?"*
>
> *Pooh looked at his two paws. He knew that one of them was the right, and he knew that when you had decided which one of them was the right, then the other one was the left, but he never could remember how to begin.*
>
> *"Well," he said slowly...*

My dad was a Marine. A center on an offensive line. And now he's like Pooh.

And when I think of him like that, I don't miss him quite so much. Because the simplicity of Pooh is well…perfect.

> "Well," said Pooh, "we keep looking for Home and not finding it, so I thought that if we looked for this Pit, we'd be sure not to find it, which would a Good Thing, because then we might find something that we weren't looking for, which might be just what we were looking for, really."

Winnie the Pooh. Perspective. And the present tense.

Thank you, Candace (and Mr. Milne), for the reminder of all three.

Here's to finding something I wasn't looking for, living in the present, and embracing

the simplicity of what is.

In appreciation of this perfect trifecta,

Juli

SO NOW WHAT?

And then we might find something we weren't looking for. What have you found that you weren't looking for in this new present tense? Sometimes you really have to look hard, but I promise it's there…something new that wasn't there before.

March 20

COFFEE WITH CANDACE

"I thought we were going on a road trip. What happened?"

"You. You are what happened."

"Oh, yes…"

"And let's be clear: There isn't a 'we.' There is a 'me' and a 'you.'"

"Oh, my word. This world is so consumed with pronouns! You, me, we…Face it: We are an 'us' now. Two peas in a pod. 'Til death do us part. Shirley to my Laverne."

"I find you tedious."

"No, you don't; you're just tired of me. Treatment is tedious; I'm more exhausting."

"Yes. You are. Exhausting. "

"Oh, come on! There is light at the end of the tunnel!"

"I'm sick of this fucking tunnel."

"Indeed. But you haven't answered my question. Why are we not Thelma and Louise-ing down 65 south?"

"Because I'm not Thelma anymore. And you, my friend, are no Louise."

"I knew you secretly considered me a friend. But still, what gives? You miss your people, you could use a little sunshine, and you are running out of time to meet with the accountant."

"I just couldn't."

"Why?"

"Because I'm not me anymore. At least I'm not the me I was three months ago. I don't know this person. I don't trust this person. I don't really like this person."

"Oh. That's where we are. I wondered when we'd reach this point."

"What point?"

"The moment you realize that everything is now quite and irrevocably different. That's part of my charm. I sweep in and rearrange everything. I'm quite subtle. Stealth-like."

"You are! I hadn't noticed at first. The changes were almost imperceptible, like the earth spinning. But now that I have space, I see that you have picked up every scrap of my life and repositioned it. And no matter how hard I try, I cannot move it back."

"No. You can't. This is your new life."

"I liked my old life."

"But it's gone. C'est la vie! Time to move on. The new you with soon-to-be new boobs. What's done is done. You are not that person anymore."

"Damn. You really are good at this game, aren't you?"

"I really am."

"I would be better equipped to challenge you if I had estrogen. With full access to my hormones, you would not be winning."

"Oh, my friend, I don't care if I win. The fun is in the journey, not the destination. And I, for one, am having a splendid time. I suggest you find some peace with this new you."

"I'm working on it."

"No rush on my end. I'm here for the long haul."

"Apparently."

SO NOW WHAT?

Two steps forward, three steps back. If you haven't cussed out your OHM, what are you waiting for? She isn't going to pack up and leave if you do. If only…

March 22

I said "Yes" to the dress!

Or in my case, boobs of silicone. Tom-a-to, to-mah-to.

I am a child of the seventies. *Free to Be You and Me* was the soundtrack of my childhood, surrounded by women who burned bras.

I didn't have Barbies because my mom didn't want me to think I would be blonde, tall, and perfectly boobed. I had rag dolls.

So it never occurred to me to change what the good Lord gave me. Of course, I bitched about my hips, my cellulite, even the weird side boobs my first round of menopause granted, but I didn't think I could do anything about it.

Until Candace!

This whole plastic surgery, body reconstruction, new boob thing has been…a thing.

But Doogie keeps reminding me that this is the fun part.

Bless him.

Actually, my last appointment with him was kind of fun. At least funny.

In he comes with three different implants. To feel. Although to date I have never actually felt up my own boobs, nonetheless, I obliged.

Basically, there are Target implants, Nordstrom implants, and Cartier implants.

Ryan keeps telling me, "This is like getting a new roof."

So Cartier it is.

Go big or go home. Or in my case, go small and expensive.

After all, once it's done, it's done.

Which actually Doogie would call bullshit on. He said most women come in and get them tweaked. *What the fuck?* Not only did I not think I'd ever get new boobs, I certainly didn't think I could "tweak" them. What a world this is!

After I chose the level, I had to determine the size. Which should be easy. We all know the alphanumerical system of bra-sizing. (Even middle school boys know this information.)

Oddly, implants don't come that way. They come by cubic centimeters (cc) level.

Again. *What the fuck?*

These are the same people who, when asked for directions, say, "go *south* at the light."

"Is that right or left, Magellan?"

I folded at 375 cc. But. That is on top of the square expanders, so in order to adequately create a mirror image of 375 cc atop plastic, Doogie will have to come into surgery with three different sizes.

Apparently, this is how it works:

1. He will pick a side.

2. Out with the expander, in with the implant.

3. "Baste stitch" my skin.

4. *Sit me up.*

5. Look at both boobs.

6. Determine if they are "even."

7. If not, he'll try another size.

8. Until perfect balance is achieved.

9. Then firmly stitch them into place.

Thank God I'm going to be asleep. I'm already mortified.

I was like, *"Shit, why don't you just have Ryan scrub in. He can help."*

For fuck's sake.

And what size bra will I buy when all of this is said and done? ← *(Seriously, why can't they figure this out?)*

I have no earthly idea.

Except, I won't have nipples. So maybe I will just go braless. ///

I'm sure my children will love that.

Juli

P.S. I think my plastic surgeon is fabulous. I mean no disrespect to him. He is a child *(at least to me)*. But a very good doctor and truly the happiest doctor I get to see. While my visits to him aren't fun, they do remind me that I'm still a person who just happens to have (had) cancer. And that's worth a million dollars.

SO NOW WHAT?

Hard things. Uncomfortable things. Things you never thought you'd experience. Yet here you are, doing it. How does it make you feel to know you are doing it? I, for one, am proud of you. But it's way more important for you to be proud of yourself.

March 24

Dear Candace,

This morning, I laughed. At a fart. This is what happens after years with middle schoolers. Farts become funny.

And it's very nice to laugh.

My week consisted of:

- Striking a balance between having a pity party and putting on my Big Girl pants.

- Fighting loneliness while needing to be alone.

- Embracing that parenthood is nothing more than a leap of faith.

- Not resenting the *hours* I spend resetting passwords to Netflix, Hulu, and Disney Plus so that my children can watch anything, anywhere, anytime.

- Finding the simple joys of Ohio in March. Which is quite gray, a little odd, but somehow beautiful.

- Giggling that I don't trust the medicine from the world-renowned oncologist but take without pause the herbs the acupuncturist gave me.

- Realizing that I'm up to me. Coop's up to Coop. Doodle to Doodle, and Ryan to Ryan. And it's *always* been that way.

- Surrendering.

Juli

SO NOW WHAT?

Have you learned that it's all about surrendering yet? It is. And I don't say that lightly. Surrendering is hard. Very, very hard. But I kinda think it's also the main ingredient in healing. What do you surrender and to whom?

March 27

Dear Nashville,

Today, my heart breaks for you.

Children.

They were children who went to school. Nothing more.

Teachers.

They were teachers who went to school. Nothing more.

I have spent the last three months thinking about mortality and fighting Death. And all those humans did was go to school. On a Monday. On a beautiful spring day.

Nashville is magical in the spring.

And, today, it was stained.

That breaks my heart.

Sing a song of peace, Music City.

I will forever think of you as a home,

Juli

P.S. I found it to be very easy to sink into my own world and into my own pain. There is a level of selfishness that needs to occur in order to fully heal, but don't lose yourself entirely. The world is, indeed, still spinning around you. Some of it good, some not so good, some downright heartbreaking, but it's still spinning nonetheless. Make sure you rejoin when you can!

SO NOW WHAT?

I lived in Nashville for sixteen years, taught school for seven. March 27, 2023 broke my heart, and cancer paled that day. The level of hopelessness that sends one human into a school to kill other humans is heart-wrenching. While I was absorbed in my own restoration, the world kept spinning. What's happening around you?

March 29

COFFEE WITH CANDACE

"The quiet is nice."

"You're welcome."

"I wasn't thanking you. I was just noticing. This time between operations is nice. I mean, you're still here, but you aren't quite as annoying."

"This is an important time. Sleeping. Walking. Breathing. Having hard conversations. All part of the treatment."

"That's good. Because I haven't been doing much else. Other than pining for estrogen."

"Yes you have. You're taking stock. You're paying attention. You're thinking."

"I'm sad."

"That too."

"I had great plans for this week. But then. Children and teachers died, and I was reminded that you often win. I have friends facing unbearable realities and children fighting to find their way. It's already Wednesday, and I'm still just sitting here with sleeping animals at my feet talking to you. Again."

"So use this time. Now is the time to do something with your own suffering. To suffer well, so to speak."

"Suffer well? What on earth does that mean?"

"It means to take your suffering, wrap it into a ball, toss it away, and send positive energy into the universe for others. Suffer well. For those you love. Turn your suffering into strength for someone else."

"Who are you, Candace?"

"Who knows? I might be your guardian angel, or your evil twin, or the ghost of Christmas past."

"Oy vey. Why can't you ever just answer. 'Suffer well,' you say?"

"Try it."

"I'm guessing you're not going to let this go?"

"No, I'm not. This is part of the process. To heal you must:

Learn to surrender.

Find your voice.

Pay attention.

Suffer well."

"Fuck. This is hard."

"Indeed. And, remember, you have a minimum of 1,825 days to do this in. Use them wisely."

"I intend to. Soon. I hope."

At some point, I realized that Candace was probably one of my angels. When I wrote our conversations, I heard her so clearly. I've said many times that my conversations with her were the most honest conversations I was having, and I also realized that if I do not learn the lessons she was teaching, then all I had gone through was for naught.

You know the saying, There are no atheists in foxholes. Or (I'd add) on cancer wings. I consider myself a spiritual equal opportunist I became a little bit Catholic, a little bit Hindu, a little bit Buddhist, and a lot spiritualist. One of my friends shared sermons from a priest out of Detroit. I learned the concept of suffering well from him.

You have angels with you. If you don't know it yet, you will soon. Listen to them. Hear the good and the bad. And then suffer well for others. It's freeing and powerful.

SO NOW WHAT?

While you're doing hard things, you can also send love into the universe by suffering well for others. Pray, sing, meditate, write—do whatever you can to give your energy and make use of your pain. Who can you suffer well for?

"If we had no winter, the spring would not be so pleasant."

October 19, 2023 (a little break from cancer in real time...I wrote this a few months later...a reprieve of sorts...and a reminder that you will get to the other side...in time...everything in time.)

I friend just sent me a *Fuck Cancer* coloring book. It's October, so the world is awash with pink. Initially, when I opened the package, I just sort of looked at it. And then I remembered I have cancer. I'm part of the very big and growing number of women worldwide who have breast cancer. I just don't think of myself as a breast cancer patient.

When a friend of mine was going through her divorce, she said that this was one of the hardest things—thinking of herself as a divorcée.

Maybe this is a sign that some healing has taken place.

I used to feel like I had a lot of answers and a lot of things figured out. I realize now that I do not. What I have is faith. Faith that I will continue to heal. Faith that I will be around to witness my children find their footing. Faith that I am a better person having experienced January to June 2023.

While I do not believe that I did something to cause cancer, I do believe that for me, cancer gave me a much-needed moment to pause and reassess. It forced me to write with an honesty that had been too frightening before. It forced me to release control of life's outcomes. (Still working on this

March

one…) It forced me to do so many things that made me uncomfortable. And while I sometimes forget, it is now a part of my story.

I have a hard time referring to my tête-à-tête with Candace as a time of healing. I wasn't sick. Sure, I had to heal from surgery, but prior to my diagnosis, I wasn't sick.

The word "restoration" resonated with me in a way that healing never did. Because while I wasn't sick, I had strayed. I didn't do anything wrong; I just lost a little bit of myself here and there. Bit by bit. Somewhere along the way, I stopped speaking my truth. Somewhere along the way, I looked to other people for answers rather than within. Somewhere along the way, I stopped listening to my angels.

Breast cancer asked a lot of me, and I gave in body parts and tears, but it also gave me a chance to restore.

I am a mom. I am a wife. I am a daughter. I am a sister. I am a friend. I am scared of what the future holds, and yet I am strong enough to face it. I am sad that the world seems to be in tatters, and yet I can only control what I can control.

I get to add to my chapters every morning. I have a say in how my story is written and how I will feel when it comes to a close.

And so do you.

Spring really means nothing if winter hadn't happened.

April

"The sweet, small, clumsy feet of April came into the ragged meadow of my soul."

—E. E. Cummings

April 4

Dear Diary,

> *To sit vigil means to stay in a place and quietly wait and pray for a period of time.*

Yesterday, I sat vigil with my parents. For their sweet dog, Doc.

But it occurred to me that I've been sitting vigil for months.

Since my diagnosis, I've been quietly waiting and praying.

While I continue to sit vigil for Doc, for my children, for Ryan, for my parents, for my friends, for my extended family, I want to thank you for subscribing and supporting this.

If you're new, let me catch you up. I'm a middle-aged woman trying to find balance (in this fucked-up world) between children launching, parents aging, and cancer. The 53-year-old trifecta!

Apologies that my letters have been sporadic.

Brain fog is a real and miserable side effect of cancer. But today, I had a pre-op appointment for my last operation! There is an end in sight (at least for this phase of the fun).

Today, while I sat vigil, this is what I pondered:

- The irony of medical professionals. When reviewing my medical history, it always makes me chuckle when asked, "Anything else?" "Other than cancer? No. Just that."

- The fact that my phone automatically writes the word "diarrhea" when I begin typing any word that begins with the letters "d-i-." And yet, every time I try and type the word "fucking," it changes it to "ducking." True, I do text about diarrhea more than the average Joe, but there is no way I type it more than the word "fucking."

Still happens!

- The hilarity that I have seen a medical specialist once a week since December 15, but somehow it was still necessary to meet the sweet Dr. Scott today to be cleared for surgery. But don't worry, there's nothing amiss with our medical system.

This is my prayer today.

> *May Doc find peace soon.*
>
> *May my mom find some as well.*
>
> *May the sun be shining in your corner of the world,*
>
> *with forsythia, daffodils, and hints of spring.*
>
> *May you know my gratitude and my appreciation!*
>
> *May you be granted the ability to type only words of your choosing,*
>
> *And may your moments of sitting vigil bring you into balance.*

With love and ironic joy,

me

April

SO NOW WHAT?

I used to think that there were rules to praying...but I don't think so now. Nor do I really think it matters who you pray to. There's power in sending your intentions into the universe. I'm sure you've found yourself sitting vigil. What are your prayers?

April 7

Dear Mary,

I like to think of myself as a cactus or a succulent. But I'm not.

I'm more of an orchid.

Not the beauty of an orchid; rather, the neediness of an orchid.

That's me. Now. A needy, fucking orchid.

These days, I am a precious, delicate, precarious being. (Thank you, Candace).

One tiny, slight adjustment to my herbs/supplements/western medicine throws me asunder.

The only other humans I know who maintain such an intricate dance with their hormones are the two humans I birthed. (God bless Ryan.)

I've been in bed for two days from the smallest of hormonal tweaks, and you, Mary, woke up one day and were told, "You will now have a baby, and that baby will be so important, he will save the world, and you won't even get to have sex. But. You will bear witness to his torture and crucifixion and will be unable to do anything about it.

"However, he will be of very strong stock—i.e., the son of God—and after three days, he will push a giant rock away and go to Heaven. Godspeed." (Gabriel)

Clearly, neither I nor my children would have been able to accept those terms.

Had it been me, I would have said, "No. I'm sorry, good sir, but I and my future offspring are merely orchids. You clearly need a succulent for that role. Godspeed to you."

I've been praying to Mary for a couple of weeks. I'm not Catholic, but I'm assuming it's okay. I've also been speaking to angels, leaning into karma, and trying to embody Buddha.

So, there's that…

Whether you believe in her story or not, it's a great fucking story, and she's the world's greatest mom.

Mary's strength, resilience, and unconditional love offer me peace. And hope.

So, Mary, thank you for saying "Yes."

Sending extra love and badass mojo to all this weekend,

Juli

SO NOW WHAT?

It takes a lot of badass mojo to do hard things. It also takes a lot of strength, resilience, and unconditional love to achieve peace. Some days, you are an orchid, some days a succulent. Which are you today? It's okay to be either, but if you're an orchid, how can you become a succulent?

April 13

Dear Hangman,

We were granted a stay of execution.

For sweet Doc. (My parents' dog.)

We thought yesterday was the day. But. He wasn't ready.

There is something beautifully surreal about choosing when to die.

When my mom and I left for the vet yesterday, my dad (and f—ing Al) suddenly became deathly ill. This happens from time to time.

But. In our family, it's dogs before humans, so we gave Dad aspirin and left with our other deathly ill, pitiful soul.

I have to be honest. When the vet announced that it was not time for the fat lady to take the stage, my knees buckled. Did this mean Doc was saved, but D-Day had come for my dad?

But. No!

Turns out my dad is not quite ready either.

Who knows when either of them will be ready for their crossover.

However, I, for one, am *not* ready.

What I'm ready for is:

- My new boobs. Monday!

- My body to find an internal temperature and stick with it.

- My children forging new paths.

- My life with Candace as a friend rather than a Napoleonic general.

- My own stay of execution.

It was a long winter.

Cold. Gray. Bleak. Tearful. Hard. Not dead. Just quiet and lonely.

I didn't hate the quiet or the loneliness. In fact, I discovered a newfound peace and faith and belief. But it wasn't easy.

None of us get to choose when we die.

But that means we get to choose when to live. Just like I can focus on the 10 percent chance of recurrence *or* the ninety percent chance of non-recurrence.

So.

Here's to 90 percent. To the end of winter. To my (and your) stay of execution. And to changing New Year's Day from January 1 to April 1.

Let's start a petition,

Juli

SO NOW WHAT?

Winter does eventually end. But it can be really fucking cold.

> *"She turned to the sunlight*
> *And shook her yellow head,*
> *And whispered to her neighbor:*
> *'Winter is dead.'"*

Living is a choice. What do you choose today?

April 14

Dear Candace,

Monday I'm going in for my exchange surgery. Which makes me giggle every time I say it—like I'm walking into Nordstrom to exchange the jeans I bought that don't quite hit right on my hips, and don't cover my belly enough, and don't miraculously make my butt look like it did ten years ago.

Clearly, I expect a great deal from a pair of jeans. Some might say I'm a bit of a princess.

Ryan might disagree, but I think this is a new thing.

However, I love this idea of exchanging.

"Thank you, kind madam, but I would like to exchange these square pieces of plastic for soft-edged, squishy jellyfish."

Exchanging implies that you get to trade in and trade up.

In addition to my boobs, I would like to exchange:

- My checking account with literally anyone with more than $66.23. Who says writing isn't lucrative?

- President Biden with anyone younger.

- Trump with literally anyone.

- My dad's brain with anyone who doesn't have Alzheimer's.

- And the world's water supply with ice cold, low calorie, more oaky, less buttery Chardonnay.

Soon, Candace, I will exchange *you* for a soft-spoken Brit who tickles my back on demand and laughs at all of my jokes.

Until then…

I will see you first thing Monday morning. I will be the one on the gurney.

J.

SO NOW WHAT?

Wouldn't it be fabulous if we could magically make exchanges? I'd exchange my hair for Mackenzi's…and hatred for understanding. What do you want to exchange?

April 16

Dear Candace,

> *"I survived cancer only to feel further than ever from my old self, whose life had seemed so limitless."*
>
> —*someone brilliant I found on Substack*

I wish I had done more than take a screenshot because I don't know who to credit for these words. But thank you.

Amen.

I, too, have felt very far away from myself.

But now,

I'm restoring.

Restoring my faith. My belief. My hopes. My dreams. Me.

Like the prairie and my boobs, I'm a restoration in progress.

So, thank you, Candace.

You are an ass, and I'm unsure whether I like you or hate you,

But…I thank you.

Juli

SO NOW WHAT?

Along the path by my house is a sign: "Restoration in Progress." I have walked by that sign hundreds of times now. But on this day in mid-April, I realized that, like the prairie, I am a restoration in progress. The layman's definition of restoration is to make something new again. Do you see restoration happening in you? Trust me, even if you don't see it, it's happening. How is restoration happening?

April 21

Dear Alexander,

I, too, had a terrible, horrible, no good, very bad day.

Several of them, in fact.

Doogie promised me that this procedure would be much easier. And. In many ways it has been. But yesterday was shit. Literally.

While I have always thought of myself as a caregiver, I'm no nurse. I hate bodily functions, not a fan of most body parts, and find it wildly annoying that wine and hot dogs are not top of my new clean, cancer-free diet plan.

Yesterday, my terrible, horrible, no good, very bad day was all about bodily functions. Of the grossest kind.

All I could do in the end was curl up in cashmere and cry myself to sleep.

Turns out cancer isn't for the faint of heart.

It made me think of our wedding vows, which I didn't think Ryan was going to have to honor so literally.

Bless this man's heart, but he has metaphorically held my hair back while I puked for years. For richer, for poorer. In sickness, and in health.

He did not sign up for this. Then again, neither did I.

But when we really love someone, we clean up their poop. That's what we do. We walk around with poop bags. Literally and metaphorically.

Thank you, Ryan, for always having a poop bag in your pocket.

And while yesterday was a terrible, horrible, no good, very bad day. Yesterday could very well have been a terrible, horrible, no good, very bad day in Australia, as well. And somehow that makes me feel better.

J.

I published my first book, Maggi and Milo, in 2016. My editor was fabulously supportive, and then she moved to Australia! It was never the success I had envisioned—probably because she moved to Australia! This and my sweet student will always make me think of Alexander.

SO NOW WHAT?

I had an eighth grader on the spectrum who sang Alexander Hamilton every time I called on another student named Alexander. I loved that child (both of them). In fact, I've been thinking a lot about my middle school students. I miss them. There is something incredibly special about a child who will just break out into song because she hears a name. Here's to the kids who are different! Here's to those who carry the poop bags! Who is carrying your poop bag?

April

April 23

COFFEE WITH CANDACE

"I think we're almost done."

"Really? Done with what?"

"With you. This. Us. This chapter. It's almost time to turn the page."

"Oh."

"Aren't you excited? You've been asking me to leave for months."

"Yes. But…oh, I don't know. What's the word for how I'm feeling? Apprehension?

Anxiety? Anticipation?"

"That's some impressive alliteration. Well done."

"Thanks."

"You're welcome. But why? Aren't you proud of the you you've become? You are almost to the finish line. Mile 26. The final chord. The last stanza. The resolution."

"That's an impressive list of metaphors."

"Thank you. I've stepped up my metaphor game. But you're deflecting. What gives?"

"I'm scared. What if I can't remember the lessons I've learned? What if I just slip back into the me I was before? What if I never see Venice? What if I waste the next 1,825 days and that's all I get? What if my sacrificial boobs weren't enough to appease the cancer gods?"

"That's a lot of what-ifs."

"That's all you got? Where are your words of wisdom? Advice? Some appropriate parabolic story."

"Sorry. All out of those."

"Seriously? You're such an ass."

"And you, my liege, are no prize. But maybe you need to start asking those questions in a different way. What if you do all those things? What happens then?"

"I guess I get exactly what I fought for. One thousand eight hundred twenty-five incredibly alive days."

"And that was the point all along, wasn't it?"

"Yes. But."

"But what?"

"Just because I won this round doesn't mean I won't lose the next. I don't want to be back here."

"Well. There's no guarantee either way. At this point, you have precisely two options. You either live...Or you don't. So I suggest you write the next chapter very well."

"You wouldn't happen to have a crystal ball or a tarot deck with you?"

"No. I'm afraid not."

"Fuck. Guess I have to do this on my own."

"Not entirely. I'll be here."

"Thank you, Candace."

"No need. It's what I do."

April

SO NOW WHAT?

You're here now. Which means you're no longer there. And I'm guessing in some ways that sucks. But what are you going to do now that you're here? What will the next chapter be about? Remember, it's entirely up to you.

April 26

Dear Mayan gods,

I've started thinking of my life in increments of 1,825 days. Or five years. This is a cancer thing. As soon as you're diagnosed, your doctors start talking in terms of five-year survival rates.

It's like that old interview question.

"Where do you see yourself in five years?"

"Well, for starters, alive."

After the five-year mark, they start talking about the nine-year mark. Which makes me giggle.

"Sorry. But survival rates significantly drop off at year ten, so we'll focus on year nine. Better for our records."

That's written in my strong, British-clipped English. I don't know why. But that's how that voice sounds to me.

I can't control the voices in my head.

So…

I started thinking about things in terms of five years. Or 1,825 days.

I climbed to the top of a Mayan temple and presented the gods with my boobs in exchange for five more years.

This strange metaphor gives me peace.

I recommend finding your own metaphor. To find your peace. Because we all get shit chapters. Mine just happened to be cancer. Yours might be a divorce. Or a car wreck. Or a corporate downsize. Or a cult.

I also recommend climbing to the top of a Mayan temple.

My shit chapter has taught me that…

It's my doctors' job to focus on surviving. It's my job to focus on living.

And as soon as I get rested (I am really fucking tired), I'm going to live a great metaphor.

Or just make one up.

Here's to the next five years. May they be filled with frequent flier miles, very good wine, and expensive underwear ruined by laughter.

Metaphorically yours,

Juli

Now that I'm on the other side of things, I struggle with finding the right word to describe my restoration months. Shit chapter? Sick? Sidelined? On the IR? I know it probably doesn't feel like it now, but you'll get to the other side, and you might want to start thinking about this.

SO NOW WHAT?

What is your metaphor for the next 1,825 days? Or the next 10,325 days? What's next on your horizon? What great metaphor will your future be?

April 27

Dear Mary,

True confession.

I voted for Sarah Palin.

I liked her. Which is now pretty embarrassing. But I did. Because I could relate to her.

She was a mom and short and wore cute glasses. All necessary qualities for a VP. But then again, we had no way of knowing how far we'd fall since the McCain-Palin ticket, did we? Today, I'd even vote for Ross Perot. Is he still alive?

But, I digress. Sarah Palin…Mary…

I like Mary for the same reasons. I get Mary. I understand Mary. Or at least I understand her as much as one can relate to the mother of the Messiah.

I have found that Mary gives me an inordinate amount of peace. And strength.

Strong women give me hope. Forget the indisputable fact that the human race is 100 percent dependent upon women for its continuation. Where would we, as a society, be without moms?

Things are pretty bleak, but can you just imagine how dire things would be without someone to wipe your tears or cut the crusts off?

For all those reasons, I now pray to Mary.

And because she said "Yes" when it would have been way easier to say "No."

I have always had a strong sixth sense. It has served me well and kept me safe. But it has morphed with cancer. (Fucking cancer changes everything.)

Just before leaving Nashville, one of my ride-or-die pals took me to a medium.

It was one of the most spiritual and comforting things I've ever experienced. For she only speaks to angels. Or spirits. Or souls. Or God's messengers. Tom-a-to, to-mah-to.

She shared so many things with me that brought me peace and gave me strength for our upcoming move. But she also said "get a mammogram."

If you've never packed up a life of sixteen years—literally or figuratively—it's a lot. Suffice to say, there wasn't time for a mammogram.

Fast-forward ten months, my armpits began hurting for no apparent reason.

You know the rest of the story.

Over the last few months, I have found my praying voice and my angels. And while I have always been attuned to my sixth sense, it is now more palpable, more real.

In late March, I had another appointment with Louise.

There had been a miscommunication about date and time, and so we were a day late.

Louise told me that she had only missed an appointment with one other person. That person also had breast cancer. And her name was Candace.

For real. (Louise isn't one of my readers.)

April

Mary came to me that day. My grandmother's name is Mary. So it was she or the OG herself. But probably my grandma. *The* Mary is presumably quite busy.

After our call, I opened my front door to find a small gift bag from my neighbor. In it was a medallion of Mary and a prayer. The remarkable thing is that she had been meaning to deliver this for weeks. But life happens. So it was precisely that day, while I was on the phone with Louise, that she finally took it off her kitchen counter and left it on my front door.

The medallion says, *Mary, Our Lady of Grace.*

When I die, if I can be remembered for anything, I hope it is that I showed grace, that I gave grace, that I lived with grace.

You know, when I die in nine years.

Just kidding.

Cancer humor.

Thank you, Mary. Thank you, Candace. Thank you, Louise. Thank you, to all the women in my life who say "Yes" every day when it would be way easier to say "No."

With admiration,

Juli

SO NOW WHAT?

There is a prayer that plays on repeat in my head. In it is the line, "Help us to stand up for the hard right against the easy wrong." Amen. What hard yes can you say rather than the easy no?

April 28

Dear John Mulaney,

You went to rehab for two months.

And came out funnier than ever.

Funny. Funnier. Funniest.

Funny. More funny. Most funny.

I prefer the former.

I saw you in Nashville a few years ago. During the great Before. When we went to comedy shows unmasked and drank out of each other's glasses and were overjoyed to be amongst other humans.

You were so funny.

And then. You know. A virus snuck out of a vent. Or a bat bit. Or the apocalypse began.

And your intervention. Which of course I knew nothing about until I watched your

Boston show on Netflix.

I'm sorry you had to go to rehab. Mostly, I'm just sorry you had to change your ways because I'm sure you had a ton of fun…before…

But. I'm glad you did. And I'm really glad you did a stand-up show laughing at rehab.

And yourself. And your fucked-up-ness.

If I were funny. Or famous. Or not a middle-aged mom. I would do a live show about my own fucked-up-ness.

Instead, I write about nipple tattoos and surgical drains and lethal boobs. Because if I don't laugh about the absurdity of this nonsense, it will kill me.

I've been thinking about my own rehab as my restoration. Which is heading into its fifth month. I'm exhausted. I'm over this. And I'm also trying to laugh so that I don't cry.

Here's to your restoration, John Mulaney. And to mine!

Laugh at your fucked-up-ness, everyone. It's a lot more fun than the alternative.

Cheers!

Juli

SO NOW WHAT?

I don't think a restoration can happen without really looking at fucked-up-ness. What's yours?

May

"As full of spirit as the month of May, and as gorgeous as the sun in Midsummer."

—*William Shakespeare*

May 1

Dear Candace,

It's May.

Not going to lie. I'm overwhelmed by the thought of May. I have been waiting for May.

Pointing toward May. But now that it's here. I'm…

tired.

I'm very very tired. Life-changing tired.

I've been tired before:

After my wedding.

When everyone said, "You can't get drunk at your own wedding"—

They lied.

After the births of my children.

After each out-of-state move.

And now.

My new post-cancer/not-really-post-cancer life.

I feel like I've gone thirteen rounds with Tyson. I'm bruised, battered, still standing. But I need to sit and cry.

To cry for the crystallization of so many memories.

To cry for the mistakes I've made. The fuck-ups I can't undo.

To cry for my children.

To cry for Ryan.

To cry for the old me. And the new me.

Just in case I don't get another chance. Today, I'm going to watch the rain fall and shed

a tear or two. And say the things I need to say. To those I need to say them to.

So, Candace, thank you for reminding me of what I have to live for. I have a lot to say.

Before it's too late.

Juli

SO NOW WHAT?

What do you need to say? Like really need to say? Say it before you run out of time. Just say it. It's also really okay to cry again. There were days I did very little but cry. It's also hard to fully know this new you. Be patient and kind with yourself.

May

May 3

Dear Mackenzi,

What a long, strange trip it's been.

I remember so many tiny details about my college graduation…which is odd. Odd because my memories are so scattered, so random, so benign. Terribly strange how some things take hold and others just evaporate.

No one tells you that. You think you'll remember everything. And then one day, there are just some memories left.

I suppose my own memories have been usurped by my memories of you and Coop.

Sunday you will graduate from The Ohio State University.

Your future self is waiting patiently for you to walk across that stage.

And as I sit in the quiet before the hoopla, there are so many memories that float to the surface.

- You were a tiny human. My tiny, dirty human. Always filthy.

- Your imagination defied your age. And marveled me.

- You spoke for Cooper when he could not find his voice.

- You had little patience for girlish behavior and yet loved being a girrr.

- You left us for weeks of the summer without so much as a good-bye or a tear.

- You were a fierce little soccer player. So fierce, we often hid our faces from opposing parents.

- You were betrayed by your body. Early and often.

- You learned the hard way that being female is often unfair.

- You also learned the hard way that not speaking your own truth only causes heartache.

- You were very, very brave to walk away and start again.

- You reset your compass and found a new True North. With new friends. And new adventures.

And now…

You get to begin again. Again.

It's not your impressive GPA or the bullet points on your resume that will ensure success. It's you. And all that you've learned and all that you've experienced.

May you always remember from where you came and greet what is to be with grace, wild anticipation, and your very own brand of fierceness.

It has entirely been my pleasure to watch you grow up.

Thank you for replacing my memories with so many moments!

Godspeed my love,

Mom

May

SO NOW WHAT?

While I spent the winter fighting with Candace, Mackenzi finished her last semester of college. Cooper found new footing. And Ryan kept us all afloat. No matter what is happening, life keeps going on around us. Say what needs to be said. (This is one of those moments of repetition I was talking about!)

May 9

Dear Father Time,

It's funny how we use the metaphor of a book to try and wrangle structure out of our lives.

At least I do.

Close a chapter. Start a chapter.

But that metaphor is deceiving because the beauty of books is that you can always reread them. When we close a chapter in life, moments morph into memories. And that's that.

While I am so eager to close this cancer chapter, watching Mackenzi close her chapter at Ohio State is bittersweet.

And that's how it is with life chapters. Some we can't wait to end…and others we'd have go on forever.

Time does whatever the fuck it wants.

We, mere humans, are simply along for the ride.

Sometimes, where Mackenzi is concerned, I feel as if she and I are connected by some weird voodoo doll. Her hormones whack out, mine whack out. She gets a stomach ache, I get a stomach ache. She breaks out, I break out.

Yesterday, I teared up at Target when I saw the rack of Ohio State t-shirts. Just thinking about her sadness makes me sad.

But that's what really great chapters do. They make us incredibly happy and then incredibly sad. Or incredibly sad and then incredibly happy.

So my advice, Mackenzi, is that you can't have the happy without the sad, or the sad without the happy. And both have their place along the ride. So take stock. Take a child's pose when needed and cry when necessary.

And then…

See what the universe has up her sleeve.

Write your chapters as well as you can. And do your best to make the next better than the last.

None of us can fight you, Father Time. But I would appreciate it if you are kind to my sad graduate.

Juli

I recently bought a new watch, and it ticks loudly, which is good and bad. Good because it reminds me that time is ticking on and my fat lady has yet to sing. Bad because time is such a hard concept for me to understand. Ahem

SO NOW WHAT?

Father Time is an elusive son of a bitch, isn't he? One of the hardest things for me to grapple with is the passing of time. How do you feel about time as you go through your OHM? Write a letter to Father Time. Let him know what you're feeling.

May 15

Dear Cooper and Mackenzi,

First, let me say thank you. For the flowers. For yesterday.

But mostly, thank you for letting me be your mom. You are both incredibly talented, terribly complicated, and a little fucked up.

You are also brilliant, passionate, and ready to launch.

Not going to lie, our trip to Oz was not along a flat yellow road.

It was uphill. Icy. Slippery. And twisty.

But it was also a shit-ton of fun.

When Dad and I were on the lake last week, every spot ushered in vivid memories of your little selves. Of our family. Of some dead dogs.

Lately, I've been doing this weird memory thing (side effect of cancer).

I've been replaying my memories over and over in my mind. Like in the movies (right before someone dies).

And that's the second thing.

I'm dying.

Not today. And probably not soon.
But I am. And so are you.

Some day.

While we are living, we are also dying.

So get on with things. Get on with becoming the person you most want to be. Don't waste any time. Because some unknown day in the future, you *will* die. Or the world will freak out about a virus. Or you will get cancer.

Third, you should know that you have very little control over *anything*. The only thing you can control is how you treat other humans, animals, and yourselves.

Some Words of Wisdom that I've collected over these last five months:

- When you drink wine, drink good wine.

- If you meet someone and he or she doesn't own books? Walk away.

- You have angels all around you. Listen for them. Talk to them. Cuss them out. But trust them.

- Life will throw way more curveballs than fastballs. Learn to adjust.

- Always have a pet.

- You can do hard things. I had forgotten that I could. But I just did. And so can you.

- And when your rudder falls off—and it will—pick up an oar and paddle. Forward. Keep going forward. Until shit makes sense again.

Never, ever, ever, ever give up, nor forget that you are loved beyond measure. You will always have a soft place to land with us.

Love,

Mom

SO NOW WHAT?

Mother's Day. I made it to Mother's Day. Being a mom is the biggest part of who I am. There is a theme to May—say what needs to be said. Now. Today. To whoever it needs to be said to.

May 17

Dear CJ,

When we first moved to Tennessee, I got pneumonia. Three times. The third time, my doctor asked, "Do you have a cat?"

"Two actually. Why?"

(Not going to lie, by this point in our relationship, I was questioning her training.)

She replied, "To finally kick this, you need to sleep every time your cat sleeps."

This.

Was her fucking advice.

Never mind that I had two elementary school-aged children, a traveling husband, and lived in a state where I knew no one. This is the script she sent me home with.

Sleep when your cat sleeps.

Somehow, I managed to do it. I laid on the couch and stared at my cats. And when one slept, I slept.

Cats sleep all the fucking time. As a cat owner, you know this, but it's not until you actually *watch* them that you realize the *hours* of impressive laziness.

To her credit, ten days later, my pneumonia was gone, never to return.

This morning as I begrudgingly dragged myself out of bed, I remembered her witchcraft cure. And then I started thinking about the universe and how weirdly perfect it all works if we just get out of the way and let her do her thing.

We adopted CJ because Coop was having an existential crisis.

Turns out Coop was fine. He just needed a five-week European vacation.

It was me who needed this silly cat. CJ the cancer cat.

I wonder how many hours CJ and I have slept since my first operation. Like his predecessors, CJ is impressively lazy. He's also kind of a jerk. Mostly to Ryan, which secretly makes me happy as all of the other animals that I walk, feed, and coddle have imprinted upon him. (Which is bullshit. But. C'est la vie.)

I felt like shit yesterday. That's a cancer thing. You string three to four good days together. And then. *Bam.* Back to bed.

So, my sweet, orange jerk of a cat, thank you for sleeping with me. And if you imprint upon Ryan one day, I will never forgive you.

Until then,

Mother J.

SO NOW WHAT?

Just because you're spiritual and almost "restored" doesn't mean you can't call an asshole an asshole or sleep when you need to sleep. Remember, this restoration thing is a marathon. So who is the asshole today? Write it down, then go take a nap.

May

May 19

Dear Candace,

You do seem to be the gift that keeps on giving!

I appreciate the respite.

We had graduation, a couple of days on the boat and several sunny days strung together.

Thank you for taking the backseat.

But now you're back.

Doctor appointments and schedules and new medications. I would like to say, "F you."

And get on with living…but…alas…it appears you will forever be with me.

Yesterday when I left Doogie's office, the sweet child nurse gave me a registration/warranty card.

FOR MY BOOBS!   *This is for real!*

Wouldn't it be nice if our real body parts came with a fucking warranty?

Not only is my chest cavity registered at what I can only assume is the *National Registry of Perkiness,* but I've been *chipped.*

My boobs can be tracked! Or at least identified in the case of armageddon or spontaneous rapture.

I feel so empowered! (Even though my cancer cat from the humane shelter of some southern Ohio farmland is *also* chipped.)

This is like an insurance policy. A Captain America shield. Wonder Woman shit.

So, thank you, Candace, for my boobs of steel. Potential abductors, be forewarned! My boobs, while perky and scarred, are also my own Bondian sensor.

I have always wanted to be a Bond girl. And now I am!

Thank you.

Juli

SO NOW WHAT?

Gifts come in the unlikeliest of places. What have you been gifted? And believe me, sometimes it's super hard to see a gift, I get it…but there have been gifts bestowed from the unlikeliest of places…

May

May 24

Dear Estrogen,

Oh, how I miss thee.

Some things in life we just take for granted.

Spring. Idiot politicians. Silly British Royals.

And our bodies producing the basics. Like hormones. Our bodies' internal batteries.

Hormones have fucked with my life more than the average Joe's. Mackenzi went through menopause at fifteen. Cooper went through a mid-life crisis at twenty-one. I got cancer at fifty-two. (All hail, Ryan! It's been a lot.)

And yet, I'd give away one of my pets for a smidgeon of estrogen.

You tried to kill me.

But…

Without you, the backs of my knees sweat profusely, I find it difficult to speak without stumbling, and I smell. Which is brutally unkind. As any middle school teacher will tell you, no one wants to sit beside the stinky, hormonal kid who hasn't yet been taught the value of deodorant. And now, motherfucker, that's *me*. The stinky hormonal kid.

Yesterday, my sweet functional medicine doctor recommended sleep, breathing, and a walk in the woods.

Bless her.

I'm like a drug addict…I just need a teeny, tiny hit. Of pure hormonal girl power.

Now that I am officially in the "healing phase" of this cancer thing, I've entered the mad stage.

Not going to lie, I'm pissed off that the one integral female element I was granted attempted a coup within the body part personally bestowed upon me as my reward for surviving puberty.

I've read a lot of shit about breast cancer, but someone needs to start saying the brutal truth. *Hormone-fed breast cancer is the cruelest of ironies.* And the gift that keeps on giving. Candace, you are an asshole of epic proportions.

And, you, estrogen, my long-standing nemesis, I detest you. But I also miss you oh so much.

J.

SO NOW WHAT?

What do you miss the most? I still miss estrogen, but I also miss having too much wine, staying up too late, and not thinking about my boobs. What about you? I'm sure you've had to give up something. Probably several things.

May

May 31

Dear Candace,

I've been in a fog. Can't pray. Can't meditate. Can't still the hamster wheel.

I'm healed. And, yet, I'm not. Quite.

Yesterday I took a yoga class. My first since diagnosis.

I started practicing yoga after Mackenzi was born. Twenty-three years ago. On VHS. *Yoga for Weight Loss.* In my naivety of thirty, I thought yoga was for losing weight. Silly me.

Yesterday kicked my ass. The slowest, quietest, most soul-comforting class ever, and I was exhausted.

Could have been the weekend of drinking and celebrating and watching baseball. All the old me things.

New me is hard to figure out.

I want to drink too much wine. I want to sit in the sun and watch nine innings of baseball. I want to stay up late and hang out with my kids.

But. Fuck. I also do not want to forget any of the lessons you brought, C.

I never want to know you again and I also have no idea how to live without you. And that's the truest thing I can think of to write.

I hate you. I thank you. I want you to move on. I need a playbook for what comes next. I am trying to hear you. For months, you were really fucking loud but now you're rather quiet.

I know I've told you to fuck off more than my fair share—and to be clear, you're still an asshole. But would you mind hanging around a bit? Behind the curtain, but…around. For just a bit longer. I'm not quite strong enough to find balance between my Yin and my Yang. Yet.

Juli

SO NOW WHAT?

There are tectonic plates that are, have been, and will continue to shift beneath you. It is incredibly hard to find your sea legs, and sometimes you have to cling to the thing you hate (but know) in order to find a new balance. What is tugging at your new Yin and Yang?

May

Three Words
(that became three new words)

Dear You,

Whoever you are, whoever you want to be, whoever you believe yourself to be…I appreciate you.

Looking back on the last five months…

In addition to the brilliantly placed "fuck," there are three words that I wrote over and over and over.

Balance.

    Time.

        Listen.

Having breast cancer forces a woman to re-evaluate everything.

You know the stats:

1 in 8 women.

220 million women worldwide. *Will be* diagnosed in 2023.

But these are the realities of those stats:

1 in 8 are still mothers. wives. daughters. sisters. friends.

1 in 8 will have to decide if she can live with an elective amputation.

1 in 8 will have to find peace in knowing that recurrence can happen at any moment.

1 in 8 will have to sit silently while her children and partner find their own voices.

1 in 8 will have to come to terms with the reality that living and surviving are not synonymous.

1 in 8 will need to learn to listen. Listen to doctors, angels, herself, and all those she loves.

It's a Sunday morning in June.

Now when people ask how I'm doing, I can honestly say that I am good. Better. Getting there.

But. This I have learned. *Balance* is really fucking hard to achieve. *Time* is the most elusive and powerful of substances. And *listening* is wildly underrated.

I'm on the other side of things. The 1,825 days begin now…and…in order to find balance, and understand time, I must listen.

Listen to what my children are saying with their eyes. Their body language. Their reactions.

Listen when Ryan quietly reaches for my hand.

Listen when I see a hawk, the beauty of a Tennessee lake, the snow fall, and the budding of spring.

Listen.

And kneel reverently when you light a fire…

Juli

Thank you.

Your conversations. Your letters. Your stories. Your prayers.

Thank you for writing them down. For saying what needs to be said. I hope you felt better for the experience.

There is not a finish line to restoration. I didn't wake up on Memorial Day suddenly healed, but I did learn so, so much.

I found my voice and began the very hard process of saying what needs to be said.

Arukah is a Hebrew word that means "complete healing or restoration, including physical, mental, and spiritual."

Here's to your *arukah* and to mine!

Reach out. Share your stories.

I have been and continue to root for you.

Love,

Juli

An After- After-Thought.

Ordeals of Huge Magnitude take months, maybe even years, to integrate. I am learning this the hard way and every time I have a setback, I feel like I've been punched in the gut. Because lessons are hard. And restoration takes time.

My three words—balance, time, listen—have become three new words: So now what?

I'm still trying to find balance. I'm still overwhelmed by the passage of time. And I'm working very hard to listen. But I'm also focusing every day on what comes next.

Like you, this is my story to pen. I get to answer this question every day in my own way. Write your next chapter well. Choose to live, not survive. Cuss when necessary, nap when needed, and from time to time, take a child's pose.

Juli